0129475374

An Essential Guide to Owning a...
Chinchilla

Mirella Poli

Designed by David Downing
Printed in China through PrintWorks Int. Ltd

CONTENTS

ACKNOWLEDGEMENTS

I would like to thank all those people who have given their time to help illustrate the book with different photographs, they are: Joanne Bernstein, Sabine Cremer, Paul Hodgson & Tara Bambury, Marty Hull, Danica Jackson, Charles Larsen, Angele & Meisha Lau, Davin Manky, Andreas Perlitz, Kelly Lynn Smith, Dunja Valdez and Audie Vaughn. Appreciation also goes to Chinchillas.com for information from their web-site regarding genetics.

Also my gratitude extends to my proof-reader Jenny North and the publishers for giving me the opportunity in printing my work.

I would like to specially thank my veterinary surgeon, Tom Mowlem and his staff at Companion Care, who have been brilliant in looking after Cheeky my chinchilla, I just wish I found him in time for Sweetie, as in my eyes he is the best chinchilla vet I have ever come across.

Finally, a big thank you goes to my family especially my Dad for always being there and friends near and far who have continued to support me.

INTRODUCTION

Since chinchillas are becoming more popular as pets, the author of this book has put together an up-to-date comprehensive chinchilla guide for those who are thinking of buying a chinchilla as a pet and for those who already own a chinchilla.

The author has gained expert experience of owning chinchillas of her own and problems that may occur during their lifetime.

Over the years more colour mutations have been introduced through 'in-breeding', this book will illustrate 21 different chinchilla colours which are confirmed by photographs, therefore making it one of the most up-to-date chinchilla books on the present market.

The book also covers ever aspect from buying a chinchilla to breeding chinchillas and includes an extensive yet useful health guide of over 60 different illnesses to look out for.

Together with over 140 photographs this book is a must for all potential and present chinchilla owners and will act as an invaluable guide to ensure a chinchilla's optimal health.

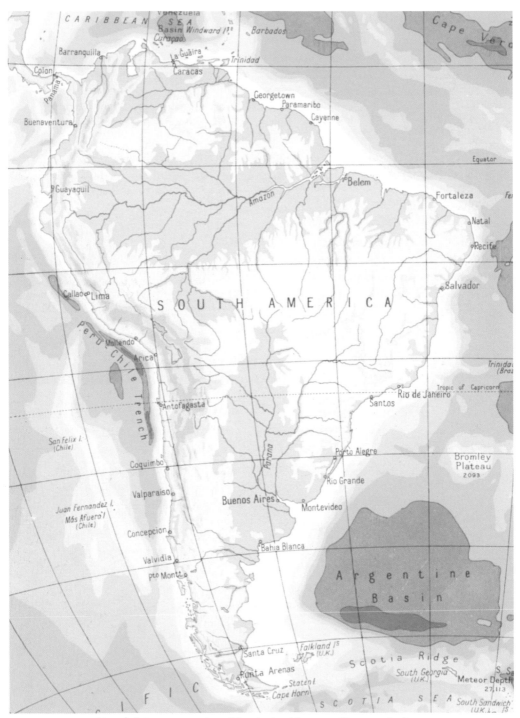

*Chinchilla's originate from The Andes Mountain Range, which are
situated along the western side of South America.*

ORIGINATION

Chinchilla's originate from the Cordillera de Los Andes (The Andes Mountain Range) which are situated along the western side of South America. The mountain range is vast, covering 5,500 miles (8,851kilomiters) and various countries such as Peru, Bolivia, Ecuador, Colombia and Chile.

The Rio Juncal Valley, where Chapman and his men searched for chinchillas.

The chinchilla's habitat ranges from 3.000 feet to 15,000 feet (914 to 4,572meters) above sea level, where humidity is low along the western side of the Andes facing the Pacific Ocean.

Due to the high altitude where they live, the atmosphere of the Andes is very harsh. The region is dry, rocky, cold and sparse with only seeds, grass, shrubs and particular cacti growing. The mountain is covered with volcanic ash and passing winds and clouds influence the temperature considerably during the day and night.

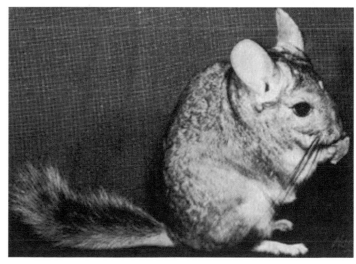

A Costina breed of chinchilla caught by Chapman.

Chinchilla's lived in the Andes within colonies of 14 - 100 for protection. They would sleep in the rocks and caves during the day, helping them to stay out of the heat and sunlight, exploring at night when it is much cooler and safer to find food.

Their diet is very bland, mainly feeding off the roots and berries off shrubs, seeds, grass and hay found around the area and drinking water from the dew on rocks or shrubs. Their thick fur would help them retain water and shield them from the cold temperatures of the night.

Their enemies were owls, snakes, hawks, mountain lions and foxes until the pelt trade took off!

M. F. Chapman searching for chinchillas in the High Andes (1920).

In the 1500's Spanish explorers came and captured as many chinchilla's as possible and began using their soft fur to make items of clothing for the rich. Many Spaniards tried to capture the chinchillas in the hope that they could take them to Spain for breeding. This would mean that the Spaniards could breed a continual herd of chinchilla, ready for the pelt trade. All attempts failed as the chinchillas died in transportation one by one due to the quick change in climate and environment.

It was not until 1918 that a mining engineer named Mathias F. Chapman saw his first chinchilla whilst visiting the Andes and fell in love with the small furry bundles of fluff which had been sold to him by a local Indian.

The story goes that he wanted to try and create his own herd but knew of the failed attempts before him. Chapman also knew that since the 1920's chinchillas had been placed on

A chinchilla called Pete often sat on Chapman's shoulder as he tended the rest of the herd.

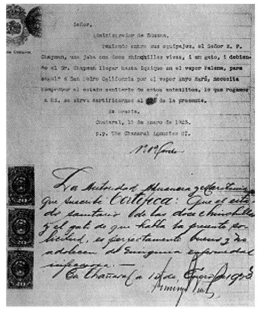

Official document regarding Government approval for chinchilla export on 15th January 1923.

an endangered species list by most South American governments due to the pelt trade causing near extinction and were now protected by law.

Chapman decided to approach the Chilean government and apply for permission to capture some of these animals and transport them to mainland America. After much persistence, the Chilean government gave Chapman permission for the task and Chapman with his band of 23 men ventured into the mountains to try and catch as many chinchillas as possible.

Chapman was hopeful his plan would work. The region in Chile was perfect for the chinchillas but to shock them into a new climate would have proven fatal for most so the progress had to be slow. He understood that the chinchillas needed time to acclimatise to their new surroundings so he planned for this allowance.

I am not too sure if he realised just how slow it would be as it took his 23 mon, 3 yoaro from 1919 to 1922 to oatoh juot 11 ohinohillao! but thio wao enough to start a colony of his own, as 3 of the chinchillas were females.

Chapman had made cages for the chinchillas that were airy and cool and

Dona Inez Suez, the finest of Chapman's captured chinchillas.

made sure the chinchillas were kept out of the sunlight during daytime hours. He collected berries, seeds, bark, roots etc. from their natural environment and continued to feed them this until he could copy their food resources back home.

They started their 10,000ft (3,048 meters) mountain decent in 1922, reaching the bottom 12 months later! Their trip was slow to ensure the chinchillas would adjust to the variations in altitude and so far the plan had worked as most past attempts had failed by this stage.

Chapman & his wife, with a crate containing all captured chinchillas awaiting shipment in 1923.

The chinchillas together with Chapman and his wife were then transported to the coast by railroad where they embarked on a coastal steamer to Callao. The final leg of the journey was aboard a Japanese freighter for the voyage to San Pedro in California.

During the journey Chapman and his wife kept the chinchillas cool with ice compartments and wet towels over the cages. Unfortunately one chinchilla died in transport but another two were born. They arrived in California on 22nd February 1923 and finally settled in Los Angeles.

It is Chapman's chinchillas which has become the foundation stock of chinchilla farms, pets and breeding grounds, which we know of today. Who even knows, without Chapman's eleven cheeky chinchillas these poor beautiful animals may even have become completely extinct.

An early type of nesting box built by Chapman containing two chinchillas.

It is said that the eighth chinchilla that Chapman caught, nicknamed Old Hoff went on to live to 22 years old! He was named after a German blacksmith who built the original cages for shipping transport.

THE CHINCHILLA

The name Chinchilla came from a South American Indian Tribe and means "Little Chinta". There are 3 different breeds of chinchillas:

Lanigera

The Lanigera chinchilla is the most commonly found today, perhaps because they are of the best production strain. They have slimmer necklines and shoulders to the Brevicaudata, and have a more pointy-head shape. Their tails are longer which gives the illusion that they are bigger but in fact they are smaller than the Brevicaudata breed. Found within the middle ranges of the mountain areas, their original colours were from light, bluish grey to brown.

Brevicaudata

The Brevicaudata chinchilla have a broad neckline and larger shoulders than

Sweetie – Black Velvet, Female.

their cousins giving them a stockier appearance. Their fur is slightly longer and wavier than the Lanigera and their nose is blunter. Pure brevicaudatas generally have a brownish shine to their fur and are found at higher elevations of 15,000 feet above sea level.

Costina

The smallest size of the chinchilla family. The Costina has short fur and are not as compact as the Lanigera or Brevicaudata. Costinas have a slightly pointier head leading to a rat-like nose. They have longer ears and tail and are slightly more highly-strung than their cousins. In the wild they can be found in regions 3,000 feet above sea level.

Although there are three different breeds, chinchilla's all generally share similar characteristics.

The original colouring of the chinchilla was light grey to brown, which helped in the wild as they could camouflage themselves more easily among the stones against predators. Their colours have only developed through in-breeding and this is why you can see so many different variations today (see chapter on Chinchilla Colouring).

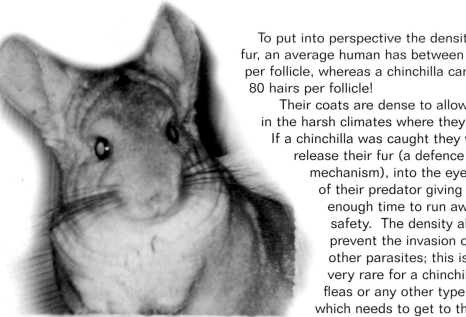

Cheeky – Hetero Beige, Male.

To put into perspective the density of their fur, an average human has between 1-3 hairs per follicle, whereas a chinchilla can have up to 80 hairs per follicle!

Their coats are dense to allow for survival in the harsh climates where they originate. If a chinchilla was caught they would release their fur (a defence mechanism), into the eyes and face of their predator giving them enough time to run away to safety. The density also helps prevent the invasion of fleas or other parasites; this is why it is very rare for a chinchilla to obtain fleas or any other type of parasite, which needs to get to the skin surface to irritate.

They all commonly have bushy tails, which are stiff and firm helping them balance and can range between 3"-11" (7.6-28cm) long, covering up to one-third of their total body length (8 ¾"-15" (22-38cm) long). As the tail is very slim, (it looks fatter because of all that fur!), it is seriously important that you never catch or hold a chinchilla by the tip as it can easily break off. If you ever need to catch or hold a chinchilla in such a way, you must ensure you hold the tail firmly at its base.

Chinchillas have big teddy-bear black eyes (few are ruby), which are under developed due to being nocturnal. To compensate for this, a chinchilla will use its whiskers to help guide them around the environment. They create a mental-map of where things are so if they need to make a quick escape they know where they are going. If your chinchillas are anything like mine,

Schneewittchen – Wilson White, Female.

this will explain why they bump into things when you have re-arranged their toys or bang their noses when you have shut their door without them noticing.

They all have short forelimbs to help feed themselves and long hind legs to help jump great distances with agility. For such small creatures, chinchillas have been known to jump 6ft in the air! They have three toes, four flexible digits for fingers and a thumb, which are severely underdeveloped but can hold and grasp food or even your finger! Watch out because they can also have sharp nails.

Mucki – Beige, Male.

One of the chinchilla's cutest features is their lovely large round ears, which extend from the top of their head. You would have thought that their hearing must be acute and ultra-sensitive due to their size, but surprisingly its not!

If you take into consideration an average human has a hearing range from 64 - 23,000Hz; a chinchilla is not much different with a hearing range of 90 - 22,800Hz. Saying this a chinchilla will become startled if they hear a loud bang or a strange noise that they are not used to so keeping them in a quiet area is best.

The chinchilla has 20 teeth from birth, 16 molars, no canines and 4 incisors, which grow continually throughout their lifetime. It is very important that their teeth are kept short to prevent any eating disorders therefore, giving the chinchilla a pumice stone, hard apple branches and other hard toys to chew on should prevent any teeth or health issues.

Chinchillas are generally very clean animals. They like bathing in the ash of volcanic rock and are generally odourless.

They are herbivores (vegetarians) feeding in

Mocha – Brown Velvet, Female.

the wild on seeds, roots, leaves, fruits, bark and alfalfa. In captivity their main diet is made up of hay and pellets consisting of molasses, hulled oats, soybean, wheat, alfalfa, vitamins and minerals.

Their life spans over 10-15 years although it has been known for them to live up to 22 years (just look at Old Hoff - Chapman's chinchilla!) and have an average weight between 1lb - 2lb (450 - 900 grams).

Chinchillas have a heart rate of 100 beats per minute and a body temperature between 96-100 degrees Fahrenheit (35.5-38°Celsius).

Chilli – Standard Grey, Female.

Chinchilla's are sexually mature between 5-9 months with the female estrus cycle approximately every 30-40 days (but can range between 16-69 days). A female may not ovulate on each cycle but generally will have up to 3 litters per year, consisting of an average 2-3 kits per litter. The gestation period generally lasts for 111 days but can average anywhere between 109 - 120 days.

Chinchillas are cute, cuddly bundles of fluff that have feelings. They are very sensitive and nervous; therefore, this should be kept in mind when choosing a chinchilla for a pet.

Unless a chinchilla is completely trained from birth, you will find the majority of them do not like to be picked up, handled or cuddled often. They will choose to come up to you and may even spend long periods sitting next to you or even on your lap, but it is their choice. (My male seems to have a foot fetish spending ages nibbling my toes, which causes me great amusement).

They are fast, very very fast and love to leap and hop around when engaging in play.

Cohabiting chinchillas will nuzzle one another and

Boomer – White Mosaic, Male.

12

Sweetie – Black Velvet, Female & Cheeky – Hetero Beige, Male fighting with a dragon.

chat away without inhibition. They thrive on interaction from their human parents and will sulk if ignored.

THE CHINCHILLA GASTROINTESTINAL TRACT (GIT)

Chinchillas originate from the harsh barren areas of the Andes Mountains therefore their digestive systems are very efficient at making the most out of very basic foods.

Dietary deficiencies on the gastrointestinal tract (GIT) are one of the main causes of Enteritis (see Health Guide).

As chinchillas are so small, storing large amounts of coarse fibre is difficult for them therefore, fibre that is difficult to digest is quickly eliminated from the GIT, whereas digestible fibre is utilised to produce nutrients and digested slower.

The GIT is highly sensitive to the introduction of new nutrients as they have been built to digest large amounts of fibre and basic foods.

A chinchilla cannot vomit, therefore giving a chinchilla rich food will

Sweetie – Black Velvet, Female & Cheeky – Hetero Beige, Male.

13

cause overload to the digestive system and result in both diarrhoea and bloating from gas, both potentially fatal to a chinchilla.

Disorders of the GIT are generally caused by high protein or carbohydrates diets; diets low in dietary fibre, internal parasites (see Health Guide), medication or genetic inheritance.

CHINCHILLA BEHAVIOUR

Although the chinchilla is well known for their placid behaviour, their temperament can change just like ours. When a chinchilla is scared, provoked or frightened it will do any of the following:
- Hide in a dark space
- Make a loud alarm cry (see chapter on Vocal Sounds)
- Bite
- Shed fur (generally when held incorrectly)

Cheeky (Hetero Beige, Male) having a cuddle with his teddybear.

Hopefully this will not happen too often, as stress is not good for the chinchilla's health! When a chinchilla reacts in a withdrawn, frightened way, it is best to give a reassuring sound and leave it well alone to recover.

A chinchilla living on its own will require more interactions than those living in pairs. The lone chinchilla will regard you as its 'mate' and hence will need much more attention. This factor must be considered before purchasing a chinchilla, as they can not just be left in its cage in a corner of some room! If a chinchilla becomes bored it will start to bite at its own fur and will laze about seeming uninterested. This is not good for the chinchilla or its health (see Health Guide - Depression), if left to continue the symptoms can lead to behaviour problems.

In the wild, chinchillas would live in colonies of 14-100 therefore they will flourish living in a pair rather than on their own. They nuzzle one another, communicate, play and generally copy what the other is doing. By having a pair of chinchilla's they each have a constant companion and you have the chance to witness individual personalities (please note introducing a pair should be done with great caution - see chapter on Introducing Chinchillas)

They are extremely inquisitive although shy and will try to get into any 'nook and cranny' just to explore. They jump about freely in the air on all fours when in total enjoyment and bounce off walls when in complete harmony, which is completely amusing to watch.

Chinchillas are cheeky characters who will do anything (just about) for a treat and will crave constant love and attention.

They need a lot of confidence to build trust so it takes time to get to know a chinchilla and for him/her to behave in such a way that you can see their complete individual character.

A chinchilla can be described as any of the following:

C ute

H erbivores

I nquisative

N octurnal

C urious

H uggable

I ntelligent

L oveable

L oyal

A gile

Sweetie – Black Velvet, Female.

VOCAL SOUNDS OF A CHINCHILLA

Chinchillas are generally quiet little animals, although occasionally you can hear vocal sounds as they communicate to one another.

Although no one really knows the meaning of these vocal noises, constant observations made by chinchilla breeders and owners have shown that chinchillas all use the same vocal sounds to describe how they are feeling at any particular time. These suggestions are listed below:

THE BASIC CRY
This is the sound that they are born with. It is used to identify one another and let others know they are there. Each chinchilla has its own unique cry but to human ears they will all sound roughly the same.

Cheeky – Hetero Beige, Male & Sweetie – Black Velvet, Female having a conversation on the telephone.

LONG LOUD CRY SEQUENCE *(Alarm Call)*

This sound is associated with alarm. The sequence can be anything up to 20 high pitch sounds. It is an interpretation that a chinchilla is excited or agitated about something unfamiliar. It is like a warning sound for other chinchillas to be aware and was used in the wild by the "look out" chinchilla if any predators or harm was approaching.

SHORT LOUD CRY SEQUENCE *(Caution or Aggravation)*

This sound is identical to the one above only shorter and not so severe. Again it is connected to caution and agitation. Other chinchillas usually stand up on hind legs, ears alert, then scurry around and hide if they hear another chinchilla make this sound. I have found my female chinchilla can make this sound in her sleep too and also if I am making a bit too much noise during daytime hours! (Whoops!)

SHRILL SQUEAL *(Frightened or Hurt)*

You usually hear this sound if a chinchilla is frightened, hurt or being handled in the wrong way. The same volume of the squeal throughout the cry means the chinchilla is in fear. If the animal is in pain, say after bumping itself on an object, the same sound occurs but will trail off at the end. My male certainly makes this noise if he has misjudged a jump and has become frustrated or his ego has been hurt!

Sweetie - Black Velvet, Female.

HISS *(Displeasure or wanting to be left alone)*
This is the sound of displeasure and wanting to be left alone; it is usually associated with being introduced to a new mate or owner. The sound will usually last a couple of days and has been compared to the sound of a cornered cat hissing.

CHIRPY FAINT REPEATING CHATTER
(Normal Conversation)
Chinchillas chat amongst themselves or whenever they are fixated with something. The sound, which is faint and bird like, means they are talking, about what I cannot say because who really knows? My female chinchilla will mutter something every time she has a go on her pumice stone, like she is having a conversation with it between bites! Whereas, my male will hop off and do something, then jump on my shoulder, chirp something into my ear, before giving a

Cotton – Pink White, Male.

friendly nibble and running off again. He will continue this circle of events 3-4 times. What is he trying to tell me - I wish I knew?.

TEETH NOISES *(Upset or Miserable)*
When you hear the chatter of teeth sounds, usually the chinchilla is upset or miserable and wants to let you know about it. They can also grind their teeth to keep them filed and food free.

HICCUP NOISES *(Male Copulation Success)*
Watch out, this weird sound usually means your male has just mated! You will only get to hear this if you are breeding chinchillas and if you are then there could now be babies on the way, so take care! It will sound as though your male chinchilla has hiccups and the sound will continue for up to two minutes.

LOUD CLICKING NOISE *(Anger)*
This is the sound of anger and can be triggered if one chinchilla has taken a toy from another, fighting or cannot get to the food bowl because its mate is in the way. In females it can be the sound they make when they are just about to spray urine. The sound has a slight rasp to it, sounds like the word "key-key".

LOUD SQUARK
Usually heard by kits (this the name used for baby chinchillas) when communicating with their mother. It can mean they want feeding, cleaning or just some basic attention. It can be heard between mother and kit whilst they

Blacky – Black Velvet, Female.

are having a conversation or between kit siblings. A kit may let out this squawk sound if it strays away from its mother and wants to be found.

All chinchillas are individuals and yours will be too. The above descriptions are basic suggestions to what is meant by your chinchilla's vocal sounds. As you get to know a chinchilla, you will be able to identify the sounds and relate them to how they are feeling at that point of time, giving you a better understanding of your pet.

CHINCHILLA POSTURES

Observing and learning what a chinchilla's posture means is another good way of telling how your pet is feeling.

ACTION: STANDING VERY STRAIGHT AND STILL/STIFF

This stance indicates that a chinchilla has sensed something unfamiliar either a smell or noise. This unfamiliarity would indicate danger in the wild and wou cause the chinchilla to react by hiding.

REACTION: Will jump back in the cage or a safe hiding spot at any minute, it is best to reassure the chinchilla and leave it alone.

ASSOCIATED SOUND: Long loud cry sequenc

Timmy – Black Velvet, Male.

ACTION: STANDING HALF-ERECT

If a chinchilla is half standing and half sitting this generally means he is expecting something to happen or is ready to learn. This could be the best time to interact with your chinchilla and teach new words or tricks.

> **REACTION:** Potential to either interact or run back in the cage.
> **ASSOCIATED SOUND:** None.

Cheeky – Hetero Beige, Male.

ACTION: IN THE CORNER OF THE CAGE - WITHDRAWN

This position displays the posture of anxiety and the chinchilla is extremely frightened. It is best to talk calmly and reassuringly to your chinchilla if this happens and never try to pick it up to coax it. If this fails, leave the chinchilla alone to recover. This may also be a sign of relaxation, perhaps after exercising, boredom or illness.

> **REACTION:** Cowering and trying to hide in the corner of cage, if you try and put your hand near it at this time, you will cause the chinchilla to frantically run around the cage and potentially injure itself.
> **ASSOCIATED SOUND:** Teeth noises or Hiss.

ACTION: LISTLESSNESS

Lying around not doing much will mean either the chinchilla is taking a quick rest or nap, it is bored or feeling ill (see Health Guide). You should pre-empt the causes for listlessness in case it is a symptom of illness (see Health Guide), if there is no illness, see if the chinchilla has taken a rest because he/she has just finished exercising. Should none of these apply then your chinchilla is generally bored and needs interaction.

> **REACTION:** If the cause is boredom the chinchilla will appreciate some interaction at this point, providing it has not been left to get bored for too long. If interaction does not work and the chinchilla has not been performing exercises then I would suggest you examine the pet for the signs of illness (see Health Guide).
> **ASSOCIATED SOUND:** None.

ACTION: CONTINUALLY ENGROSSED IN DOING THE SAME THING

Blizzard – White/Ebony, Male.

This can be the sign of a mischievous chinchilla, therefore you should go and see what it is up to, most likely they have found a small gap and are working out ways to get through it! If a chinchilla is up to something potentially

dangerous then distract it by offering some toys and interact with him/her to take their mind off what they are doing.

REACTION: Persistently running to the same area, occasionally looking up to check where you are and 'jumpy'...definitely the signs of a mischievous chinchilla!

ASSOCIATED SOUND: Chirpy faint repeated chatter.

Rascal - Standard Grey, Male - 11 weeks old.

ACTION: WAITING AT THE CAGE DOOR

A chinchilla in this stance will be begging to be let out of its cage and is ready to play. The chinchilla will be most co-operative at this stage and eager to interact with you.

REACTION: Sitting at the front of its cage in a "begging like" stance. It's paws will be holding onto the mesh at the front of the cage.

ASSOCIATED SOUND: Short loud cry sequence.

ACTION: CLEANING HIMSELF

A chinchilla cleaning himself means he is comfortable and at home with his environment. If a chinchilla washes infront of you he is showing no inhibitions and is comfortable with your close presence. He is showing that he trusts you.

REACTION: A good old clean of those big ears and a long stretch of the whiskers.

ASSOCIATED SOUND: None.

ACTION: RUNNING UP WALLS AND AROUND FURNITURE

Chinchillas can pick up enough speed and are agile enough to run vertically across walls and furniture. When you witness this type of behaviour, they are in the midst of play. They can either be showing you their game of 'It' ('Tag') by running backwards and forwards to you or just generally showing you what they can do.

Chinchillas are extremely agile, this chin is jumping over his house backwards! Dusty – Hetero Beige, Male.

REACTIONS: Running across walls vertically.
ASSOCIATED SOUNDS: Chirpy faint repeated chatter, unless they bump into something then vocally you will hear a Shrill Squeal.

ACTION: HOPPING OR JUMPING AROUND ON ALL FOURS

This is one of the most amusing actions a chinchilla can show you, they will bounce about on all fours springing into the air. This indicates that they are playing without a 'care in the world' and you should just sit there and enjoy the show.

REACTIONS: Will jump, bounce about on all fours, springing into the air.

ASSOCIATED SOUNDS: Chirpy faint repeated chatter, unless they bump into something then vocally you will hear a Shrill Squeal.

ACTIONS: RUNNING BACKWARD AND FORWARDS INTO THE CAGE

This can be another sign of the mischievous chinchilla generally up to something that will need checking out. Usually they have found a new toy that they are trying to hide or can not make up their minds whether to stay in with their partner or come out for a runabout. This could also be a sign that the chinchilla is nervous in staying outside its cage and should be talked to gently.

REACTIONS: Constant back and forth between the cage and outside not making up his mind to stay long anywhere.

ASSOCIATED SOUNDS: Chirpy faint repeated chatter.

ACTIONS: GENERAL INQUISTIVE RUNNING AROUND

If the area has been recently cleaned, a chinchilla will explore the area to check that the belongings are back in their proper place. They are sticklers for routine! If you have moved things about, expect a slight bump on the nose but generally the chinchilla will explore the new surroundings with caution followed by gratitude for the variation.

Sweetie – Black Velvet, Female.

REACTIONS: Constant running about the area checking it out. At this stage make sure there is nothing lying about which can be dangerous, as this will be a sure time that a chinchilla will find it!

ASSOCIATED SOUNDS: Chirpy faint repeated chatter, unless they bump into something then vocally you will hear a Shrill Squeal.

ACTIONS: SNIFFING AND NIBBLING AT ONE ANOTHER

If sniffing starts at the introduction of chinchillas they are merely getting to know one another, if this is the first meeting you should be on guard in case any fighting breaks out. Sniffing and nibbling one another is a sign of affection and acceptance the same as if a

Sam – Standard Grey, Male & Snow White – Pink White, Female.

chinchilla was to come up to your nose and sniff or nibble it. An adult sniffing the nose of a kit equals acceptance from the mature chinchilla. A co-habitating male will also sniff the female at the onset of 'heat'.

REACTIONS: Lots of sniffing and nibbling.
ASSOCIAATED SOUNDS: Chirpy, faint, repeated chatter.

ACTIONS: CHEWING AND GNAWING

This chinchilla will be either trying to file his teeth or is trying to escape. Check that he is not succeeding in his freedom plan or leave him to file his teeth to wear them down.

REACTION: Gnawing and chewing of objects.
ASSOCIATED SOUNDS: Gnawing and chewing with some chirpy faint, repeated chatter.

SEXING A CHINCHILLA

Sexing a chinchilla is very difficult especially if they are young. This is because the space between the anus (which helps indicate the sex), and the genitals, is very small. It is possible for the experienced breeder but to the novice it becomes more noticeable as the kits get older.

The confusion is because the female's urethral canal (where she urinates from) extends out of the body and looks similar to a penis. As the kits grow, a male will have approx. ½" (1-1½ cm) separation between the penis and the anus, whereas, the female's urethral canal will be directly above the anus, the vaginal opening is noticeable in between the two.

The females are usually easier to identify as they hold more noticeable features than the male.

When mature, a female chinchilla will be larger than their male companions and are generally more dominant, becoming the "rulers of the roost".

They are also heavier than their male counterparts ranging from 17-21ozs (500-600 grams).

Females have six nipples spread evenly on each side of the stomach area and their sexual organs will become more noticeable during times on "heat".

It is especially important to sex a chinchilla if it is to live in a pair.

There are a few exceptions but generally two chinchillas of the same sex do not live well together, in fact, they can potentially kill one another!

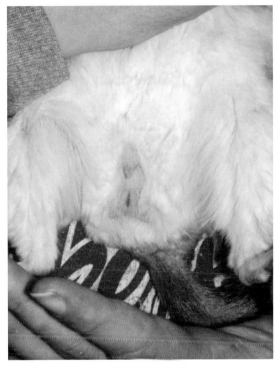

Male Chinchilla.

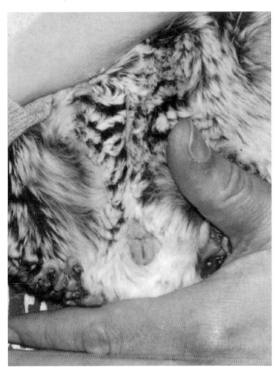

Female Chinchilla.

Chinchillas of the same sex who have been together since birth should still not be taken for granted. It is advisable that if you would like two chinchillas, you choose one of each sex.

It is also useful to mention in this section that there is a fatality gene when breeding particular colours together, the reason for this will be discussed in more detail within the Genetics chapter page 64.

Should you be looking at purchasing two chinchillas it is imperative that you read and fully understand the complications of certain colour mutations and choose not to house these two together or alternatively have the male castrated.

For now, if you are buying two chinchillas aim to pick different colours, this will help prevent any future complications.

If you are unsure as to the sex of your chinchilla, be sure to find out before introducing it to another. This is so important that it cannot be understated.

CHINCHILLA COLOURING

Before capture and in-breeding with human help back in the 1950's, the chinchilla's base colour was light grey - brown.

Today, chinchillas vary in colour (see list below) but usually they share the same characteristics as one another with mainly black eyes (occasional ruby) and a white or light grey underside (stomach).

It should be noted in this chapter that due to inbreeding to create the different colours we are about to mention, some chinchilla's have suffered slight side effects such as fur biting which is not life threatening but can become an irritant to the chinchilla.

WILSON WHITE

This was the first 'white' colour mutation born in 1955. Chinchillas are completely white with grey ears and black eyes.

WHITE MOSAIC *(commonly SILVER MOSAIC)*

Similar to the Wilson White only with scattered patches of colour not evenly spread. They all commonly have a pink nose, grey ears and black eyes. A Silver Mosaic is produced from breeding a White chinchilla with a Standard Grey.

PINK WHITE

These chinchillas have pure white fur with red or ruby eyes, pink ears and nose. Genetically produced by breeding a White chinchilla to a Homozygous Beige chinchilla.

GOLDEN MOSAIC
(or BEIGE/WHITE MOSAIC)
Same as the Pink White chinchilla only there will be scattered patches on beige highlights around the head and body. Genetically produced by breeding a White chinchilla to a Heterozygous Beige chinchilla.

WHITE VIOLET
Same as the Wilson White only with scattered Violet highlights instead of a more common grey. Black eyes and violet ears. Genetically produced by breeding a White to a Homozygous Violet chinchilla.

SILVER *(or SILVER WHITE)*
Same as Wilson White only with a more prominent even distribution of grey hair through the head, body and tail (sometimes has black tinges at ends). White belly, black eyes and grey ears. Genetically produced by breeding a White chinchilla with a Standard Grey.

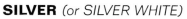

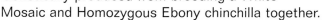

WHITE EBONY *(or TOV WHITE & BLACK/WHITE CROSS)*
Same as the Wilson White only with patches of black on either it's face and/or irregular places. They all commonly have black eyes and grey ears. Genetically produced from breeding a White Mosaic and Homozygous Ebony chinchilla together.

HOMOZYGOUS BEIGE
Homozygous Beige is similar to the Heterozygous Beige only it's coat is lighter like champagne and their eyes tend to be red rather than ruby. They have a white belly and pink feet, nose and ears. Genetically produced from breeding together Homozygous Beige to a Homozygous Beige.

HETEROZYGOUS BEIGE

This colour mutation first appeared in 1955. The coat ranges in colour from light beige to dark beige leading to a white belly. They all commonly have pink ears, feet and nose. Their eyes are ruby (slightly darker than the Homozygous Beige). Genetically produced by breeding a Standard Grey chinchilla with a Beige chinchilla.

TAN *(or BROWN & DARK PASTEL)*

The coat of this colour mutation ranges from brown to intense dark brown covering the entire body including the belly. Their eyes are red-ruby and the ears are pink. Paws range from pink - brown. Breeding together a Tan and Homozygous Ebony produces a Dark Tan, the Medium Tan is achieved by breeding a Homozygous Ebony to a Pastel.

PASTEL TAN *(or LIGHT PASTEL)*

Fur is a light beige/brown and is evenly spread across the body with a cream belly. Eyes are red. Ears, nose and paws are pink. A dark pastel is produced by breeding a Heterozygous Beige with Homozygous Ebony, to achieve a lighter pastel the Homozygous Ebony needs to be replaced with a Heterozygous Ebony.

BROWN VELVET *(or TOV BEIGE)*

Fur will display a colour of dark brown over a beige background and show the paw stripes and veiling common to the TOV breeds. They universally have a white belly, pink feet, ears and nose and ruby eyes. Genetically produced by breeding together a Heterozygous Beige and a Black Velvet.

VIOLET

First introduced in the mid-late 1960's with a soft light-grey/purple coat and a white belly. They commonly have black eyes, light-grey/purple face, nose and pink ears. Genetically produced by breeding two chinchillas with the Violet gene.

TOV VIOLET

TOV Violet chinchillas have the same characteristics as the Violet only with a darker shade of violet covering the face and running across the back and down the tail. Genetically produced by breeding a Homozygous Violet to a Black Velvet Violet carrier.

SAPPHIRE

First developed in 1963 and better seen under lighting, this colour mutation will have a light-dark blue head and body and a white belly. They have black eyes and blue/grey ears. Genetically produced by breeding two Homozygous Sapphire's together.

STANDARD GREY *(The original chinchilla colouring)*

Colours of the fur range from light-dark grey leading to a white belly. They all have black eyes. Grey feet, nose and ears. Produced by breeding two Standards Greys together.

BLACK VELVET *(GUNNING BLACK or TOV STANDARD)*

Developed in 1956, this colour mutation has an intense black topcoat on a grey background leading to a white belly. Black eyes, face, paws and dark ears.

RECESSIVE CHARCOL

First appearing in late 1950 these chinchillas had the appearance of dark grey/black coats leading to a grey belly. They have black eyes and dark ears. This colour mutation is sometimes hard to differentiate from the Heterozygous Ebony.

HETEROZYGOUS EBONY

Unlike the Homozygous Ebony this chinchilla has visible signs of grey within the coat and a grey belly. They commonly have dark ears, eyes and paws. Genetically produced by breeding together an Homozygous Ebony and Standard Grey chinchilla

HOMOZYGOUS EBONY

This colour mutation is completely black with no signs of any other colour, even it's stomach is black which is the best way to tell if a chinchilla is an ebony or ebony carrier. They feel unusually silky and their coat is more shiny than any of the other colour mutations.

ANY TOV *(TOUCH OF VELVET)*

The term TOV is generally used on any colour mutation which expresses the veiling gene to produce a darker shade across the face running down the back and tail of the chinchilla. There will also be a noticeable stripe on the front paws and are more commonly produced by breeding a Black Velvet with a specific colour. There are many different combinations such as TOV Violet (Black Velvet bred with Homozygous Violet). TOV Sapphire (Black Velvet bred with a Homozygous Sapphire), TOV White (Black Velvet bred with a White chinchilla) and so on.

CHINCHILLA AGE IN HUMAN YEARS
This chapter is just for fun and should be looked upon lightly.

We can put a chinchilla's age in relation to a humans if we assume that the average chinchilla lives approximately 10 years and humans until the average age of 76 years approximately.

Using this basis we can calculate the age of a chinchilla in relation to human years as shown below:

CHINCHILLA AGE	HUMAN AGE *(rounded up)*
1	8
2	15
3	23
4	30
5	38
6	46
7	53
8	61
9	68
10	76

This is not confirmed information and is only an approximation of how old a chinchilla could be in relation to humans however; there is a visible connection between the ages in respect to the stages of life.

Cheeky – Hetero Beige, Male & Sweetie – Black Velvet, Female.

IS A CHINCHILLA RIGHT FOR YOU?

There are many factors to consider when purchasing a chinchilla and it should be thought about carefully. The first and foremost, is whether the chinchilla is the right type of pet for you. By reading through this book you will obtain a good understanding of the chinchilla and their needs.

Please do not purchase a chinchilla because they look cute and cuddly, I have mentioned before that the majority of chinchillas do not actually like being cuddled. To achieve this the owner will have to dedicate long hours in training the animal and even then a chinchilla may still choose to decline the offer.

It should be mentioned again that chinchillas are nocturnal animals therefore, if you are looking for a pet to keep you company in the day, a chinchilla will not be your best bet. They awaken as daylight hours fade so if you like time to relax in-front of the television at night then a chinchilla will not be getting the attention and exercise it needs. This is also a good reason why chinchillas will not make excellent pets for young children. Please remember this if you are thinking of buying one for a child - it will not be a good idea!

Maggie - White Mosaic, Female - 3 weeks old.

It is debatable whether they take up a lot of space or not. Their cages should be a minimum size of 18"-24" (46-61cm) deep x 24"-36" (61-91cm) wide x 24"-36" (61-91cm) high.

If you consider how fast they run, their natural environment of the mountains and the energy they have, a cage this size without any freedom to run anywhere will cause your chinchilla to become withdrawn and be more susceptible to health issues.

Taking this into account, if you choose to purchase a chinchilla remember it either has to have a big enough cage (bigger than the one mentioned above) to live in or you will need to make provisions for it to come outside the cage for a nightly run around.

Consideration should also be given due to their long life span (usually 10-15 years) and whether they will live as a lone chinchilla or in a pair.

If you are buying just one chinchilla you must remember that it will look upon you as its mate, therefore demanding much more of your attention. If you choose a pair you also must remember that they will take up double the amount of space and at some point you will have babies, unless the male is castrated, therefore please consider your options very carefully!

So far I may have put some people off of buying a chinchilla, but in writing this book it is my responsibility not to paint just a picture of a cute bundle of fluff, especially if you are unsure if a chinchilla is the right pet for you. By informing you of the pros and cons of owning a chinchilla I am hoping that you can make an informed choice, not only for you but also for the chinchilla's well being!

I agree they are cute and desirable but I would hate to think that people only buy a chinchilla because of their looks - what would happen if they then got bored of them during their 10-15 year life span?

A PET IS NOT A PRESENT IT IS FOR LIFE

If you have carefully considered the responsibility of owning your own chinchilla and have decided to go ahead, then you will not be disappointed with your decision (if you are then you did not consider your options well enough at this stage!).

They are cute bundles of fluff, that is the only way to describe them. When they trust you they will be happy to see and play with you, they will give you great amusement when they bath and hop around on all fours. They will become very loyal to you and miss you when you are not there (some chinchillas have been known to shed their fur when their owner has gone on holiday), so which one do you choose?

Foster Mom Eileen - Standard Grey playing hide-n-seek with Jamie & Janice, Females, Violet kits, 5 weeks old.

MALE OR FEMALE?

When choosing a chinchilla the sex really does not make any difference apart from if you are thinking of introducing pairs (see chapter on Introducing Chinchillas).

There are slight physical differences such as the female being larger than the male and the difference in sex organs but apart from that no other dissimilarities in their psyche can be seen.

The temperament of both sexes is generally docile unless provoked but it is known that a female will spray urine if she becomes angry whereas a male may grunt or bite.

Females do tend to be more territorial, so maybe start with a male if you are thinking of pairing, this may make life a little easier at the introduction stages.

Males tend to be more extroverts than their female counterparts and are known to bond more easily with humans. Females tend to be more distant and take longer connecting with humans.

If you have a pair of chinchillas and are considering having one neutered against kits, then it is always best to choose the male. The castration of the male is a lot easier and quicker than for the female, therefore giving more chance of survival (see chapter on Castrating a Male Chinchilla)

*Roo - White Mosaic, Male &
Sydney - Standard Grey Female*

BUYING A CHINCHILLA

Under no circumstances should a chinchilla be purchased if it is less than 12 weeks old! This is the minimum amount of time it takes to wean a kit from its mother and if done too soon, the chinchilla can develop behavioural and health problems. It has also been known for kits to die if they are taken from their mother too soon, so please check their birth date before purchasing.

There are no differences in behaviour between the various colours so colour should not be the foremost criterion when choosing your pet.

It has been said that males do bond easier with humans than their female companions who can spray when angered but again not all chinchilla's are the same. (My female chinchilla is equally as loving as my male).

Cheeky – Hetero Beige, Male.

Tia – Standard Grey (Ebony Violet Carrier) having a cuddle with her owner.

The only reason why you would need to consider the sex when buying a chinchilla is if you were going to buy two, otherwise the only important thing to look for in a potential chinchilla is it's health.

There are a couple of choices of where to buy your chinchilla, the first being a pet shop.

Some pet shops will not display their chinchillas as they are nocturnal and do not like to be peered at. If your pet shop has chinchillas, take a look in their cage to see how they are living.

Check that the pet-shop is prepared to give you advice and help not only during the purchase but also as an aftercare advice service. Ensure that they are happy for you to handle the chinchilla under their supervision before buying it, if not; go to another pet store!

You can also buy a chinchilla from a respected breeder; this can have added benefits of seeing the chinchillas when they are awake in the evening. You can view them in their home environment (instead of only during opening hours of a busy pet shop) and also receive expert knowledge regarding a particular chinchilla from its present owner.

From whomever you decide to purchase your chinchilla, there are some important factors to look for and the best way to do this is to handle the chinchilla before paying for it.

HOLDING A CHINCHILLA

A chinchilla being supported from underneath.

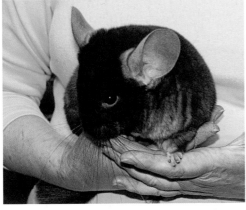

Always support the underside of a chinchilla as shown in the picture above.

Chinchillas will become frightened and hide in a corner if not approached properly. Approach the cage slowly and see if the chinchilla comes to meet you, if so, talk quietly to it until it is calm, then you can open the door.

Place your hand inside the cage and let the chinchilla come to you, do not try to grab it or it may bite in defence. Keep your hand perfectly still at this stage as any sudden movement will cause the chinchilla to panic and scurry into a corner. It will begin to sniff your fingers and after a few minutes start to trust you, if you give a chinchilla enough time it will usually jump onto your hand and start to explore your arm.

There are various ways of picking up a chinchilla but for the novice the best way (and most friendly) is to slowly and firmly scoop the chinchilla up in both hands from underneath. Be prepared, as they are quick and will most likely want to jump out of your hands straight away!

Once the chinchilla is in your hands bring it close to your chest. Your chest will then support the underside of the chinchilla, with one hand on top leaving your other free to stroke or perform an examination.

Another way of holding a chinchilla if he's facing you is to place both hands around the sides of your chinchilla and hold the tail

Alistar – 10 years old - Hetero Beige, Male.

firmly by it's base with one hand leaving the other hand free to support the animal. Never grab at the tail and never hold the tip, which will break.

For repeated behaviour, it is a good idea to give a chinchilla a small treat when putting him back down, this way he will begin to associate a treat with being picked up and this should make the process over time much more easier.

When holding a chinchilla or when a chinchilla is under examination, do not allow the feet to dangle, always ensure the feet are supported by a free hand. Once the chinchilla is comfortable you can then check it's health, any infections or signs of ill health are explained later in the book under the 'Health Guide Section'.

(The Health Guide is merely suggestions and observations from owning chinchillas and is no way a replacement for veterinary advice).

CHINCHILLA EXAMINATION

EYES
Chinchilla's eyes are generally black (occasional ruby). They should be sparkly, clear, dry and unmatted. If you see signs of weeping, stickiness, scabs or redness around the edges this is an indication of ill health.

Sparkling eyes are a sign of good health.

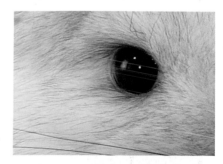

EARS
Ears of chinchillas are quite easy to look into due to their size, check that they are not weeping and that the chinchilla is not pawing at them. Touch the ears gently to ensure they are not too hot, they use their ears to cool down so hot ears could mean a temperature.

Ears should be dry and clean.

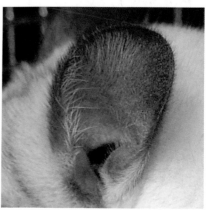

NOSE

A chinchilla's nose should be dry and clean. Check that it is not red, dry, flaky or inflamed, as this could be a sign of a fungal infection.

MOUTH

Any signs of wetness around the mouth area will generally mean there is a tooth issue. The mouth should be completely dry and clean and the chinchilla should not be pawing at its mouth.

A dry and clean nose and mouth is a good sign of a healthy chinchilla.

TEETH

Sometimes the best way to see the teeth of a chinchilla is to give them a treat. Do not be alarmed by the colour as healthy chinchillas have yellow-orange coloured teeth. Do not purchase a chinchilla if the teeth are white or a creamy colour, as this would indicate a calcium deficiency that could lead to further health issues. A vet qualified in chinchillas should always be able to check a chinchillas teeth without the need for anaesthetics.

FEET

The feet of a chinchilla should have 3 toes and should not have any cuts, scabs or sores showing.

Chinchilla's feet only have 3 fully-grown toes and 1 short stump.

ANUS

Not so pleasant but it still needs checking! The area around a chinchilla's anus should be clean and dry. If you detect matting of hair and wetness this could be a sign of diarrhoea, tooth problems or ill health.

DROPPINGS

The best way to examine the droppings is to actually pick one up. They are odourless and can vary in colour depending on what the chinchilla is fed; usually they are dark brown in colour. Droppings should be oval or rounded, smooth, plump, slightly moist and un-slimmy. When broken open a healthy dropping should have a solid consistency throughout. Holey droppings can be a sign of a digestive problem.

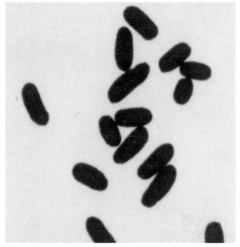

Droppings from a healthy chinchilla.

WEIGHT

A chinchilla should feel firm and compact, if you can feel bones the chinchilla could be malnourished due to an illness or a high metabolism due to hyperactivity. Males generally weigh between 14-18 ozs (400-500 grams) and females between 4-21 ozs (400-600 grams).

Sassy – Hetero Beige female weighing 2 lb.

FUR

A chinchilla's fur should be smooth, clean, untangled, dry and of even length all over (approximately 25 mm (1") long). If you see shorter patches the chinchilla maybe in the habit of biting its own fur.

Homo Ebony Male.

SETTING UP A HOME

Before you bring your new chinchilla/s home you will need to ensure you have the essentials ready for their arrival. You will also need to decide where you are going to house your chinchilla/s as this is a major factor to its continuing good health.

Top floor of chinchilla cage (built by Steve Hibbard). The home of Cheeky and Sweetie.

Bottom floor of chinchilla cage (built by Steve Hibbard). The home of Cheeky and Sweetie.

POSITION OF CAGE

For a chinchilla to feel comfortable and protected, the location of the cage is vitally important. You should never house a chinchilla outside unless you have some type of heating system in place. The fluctuations in outside temperature can be detrimental to a chinchilla's health; therefore you should choose a room that is light, airy, cool and quiet during the day, with an ideal temperature range of 60-75 degrees Fahrenheit (15.5-24°Celsius).

Never keep a chinchilla in temperatures of 75+ degrees Fahrenheit (24+°C) as the chinchilla can suffer heat stroke and die.

If you do not have a quiet room, place a sheet over the cage during the daytime as this will help calm the chinchilla and aid in sleep.

Chinchillas are happiest if kept off the ground as they like to be high up, it also helps prevent them becoming scared when you approach the cage. The best location is in a corner of a room, this way they cannot be viewed from all four sides and gives them a feeling of security.

The cage should always be kept away from radiators, draughts, sunlight (which can cause cancer to their ears) and any objects that could be in reach of the chinchilla (i.e. placing the cage next to curtains or wires).

CAGE TYPES

There are various different types and sizes of chinchilla cage, the most common being the wire bottom cage with measurements varying from 18-24" (46-61cm) deep x 24-36" (61-91cm) wide x 24-36" (61-91cm) high.

Wire Bottom Cage

Galvanised wire mesh is the most common with a ½" x ½" (12mm x 12mm) mesh bottom. This type of cage is the most hygienic for your chinchilla and is easier to clean.

Food, urine and droppings can easily pass through the mesh holes into a lined tray underneath keeping your chinchilla away from any potential infections. The tray can also be easily removed and cleaned without causing disruption to your pet.

Wire Bottom Cage.

Consequences: Chinchillas have been known to break a leg jumping on this type of floor, get sores on their feet from constantly standing on the wires or even get their foot caught in the holes.

Ensure that the flooring grids are no bigger that ½" x ½" (12mm x 12mm). The ideal would be ¼" x ¼" (6mm x 6mm) especially if your chinchillas will be having babies. A good idea is to scatter small planks of wood (untreated pine) on the floor which they can jump onto to prevent broken bones or trapped limbs.

Solid Bottom Cage

These are safer for your chinchilla and especially their babies. The bottom of the cage is detachable and is lined with untreated pine shavings or hay, which can be used as bedding to burrow into.

Consequences: With a solid base there is no where for waste to go, therefore your chinchilla will be coming into direct contact with its food and natural waste. The bottom will need to be cleaned each day to prevent infections to the chinchilla and fungus setting into the flooring. As the floor is detachable, your chinchilla will need to be placed somewhere safe whilst it is being cleaned.

Used Cages

You can use the cage of another chinchilla provided it is properly cleaned to disperse of any bacteria build-up that would be detrimental to your new pet.

Solid Bottom Cage.

You must ensure you disinfect the whole cage especially concentrating on the corners and dark areas where fungus can be growing then rinse thoroughly with fresh water. I would be inclined to do this procedure a couple of times and at least 48 hours before your new chinchilla will be housed there.

This process is easy for the wire bottom cages but the solid bottom cage tends to hold the scent of the old chinchilla no matter how much you clean it so I would advise against using this type of cage in this instance.

Solid Bottom Cage.

Home Made Cages

Thorough research must be undertaken before attempting to build your own cage and you should only try this if you are completely experienced. Many people have enjoyed the challenge but some with fatal consequences to the chinchilla.

If successful you can create a wonderful environment of any size and layout for your pet to live in but there are so many factors to take into consideration that I would seriously advise extensive research first.

Consequences: You must ensure it is

A sturdy and secured homemade cage.

completely suitable and stable for the chinchilla or it can kill them!

You must never build a chinchilla cage out of wire that is coated in plastic, chicken wire, wood other than natural untreated pine or any material which has holes larger that ½" x ½" (12mm x 12mm). Never, under any circumstance use an aquarium, your chinchilla will over heat and die!

You must also ensure the door is big enough so if the chinchillas continue to grow they will still be able to get out of the cage.

REMEMBER: TREASURE A CHINCHILLA - DON'T ENDANGER IT.

Other things to look out for when choosing a cage are protruding wires or sharp edges, which can cut a chinchilla. Additionally shelving which is not made from natural untreated pine and lack of ventilation (air circulation).

OUTDOOR CAGE

You should never house a chinchilla outside unless you have some type of heating system in place. The fluctuations in outside temperature can be detrimental to a chinchilla's health causing death if not adhered to correctly.

Should you wish to house your chinchilla outside then you will need to ensure that the environment stays at a constant temperature of 60-75 degree Fahrenheit all year round and is also safely secured so the chinchilla cannot burrow and escape.

Should a chinchilla ever escape outside the chances of catching it are very slim and he/she would be left to predators such as cats and foxes therefore if you are unsure of how safe it is do not try it!

If you are thinking of building an outside run for your chinchilla then take into consideration the poisonous plants, position of the cage in the sun, cats and dogs about and do not allow them to come into contact with the grass or pavement. Pavements carry germs that can be detrimental to your chinchilla's health and grass may be treated which could be damaging to their digestive tract if eaten.

When carrying your chinchilla to its outdoor play pen ensure you have a good grip or better still place it inside a small well ventilated box inside the house and only open the box when they are in the security of the outside playpen to ensure no escape.

Anastasia - Pink White, Female.

WOOD SHAVINGS

The best choice of wood shaving is white untreated wood; the ideal being untreated natural pine.

Newspaper can be used as lining of a wire bottom cage and hay on a solid base cage, these will need to be changed regularly to prevent mould setting in or dampness for fungus to grow.

Irritations to the eyes and nose can be caused by sawdust as well as sand, which can also absorb moisture from the air and the chinchilla's fur causing them to become dry and itchy.

Never use shavings that have come from compressed wood found in builders' supply yard as these can be made up from treated stained and glued wood and will be fatal to the chinchilla if digested.

NEVER USE Cedar, Eucalyptus and Redwood, as these too are extremely toxic and again will be fatal if digested.

CAGE HYGIENE & CARE

Cages and chinchillas are odourless providing regular duties of sanitation are performed.

Daily
Water bottles should be rinsed and replaced with fresh water (preferably boiled, then cooled) and any remaining food should be removed from the cage and discarded.

Chinchillas usually sit on the rim of their food bowl to eat and have been known to urinate into their food so fresh food should be given even if the pellets still look untouched.

Duffy and Tweety – Standards, Male and Female.

Any loose hay scattered along the cage floor should be gathered and thrown away as again it could contain urine and be digested.

Any droppings in the dust-bath should be sieved out and removed.

Once A Week
The waste from the litter tray should be disposed of and the tray sterilised with disinfectant before rinsing well with water. Ensure it is dried thoroughly to prevent fungus formation before new lining is laid.

Water bottles should be sterilized and cleaned using a bottlebrush to prevent the creation of poisonous algae, which could be digested by your chinchilla. Never use bleach or harsh disinfectants in water bottles, a tiny amount of washing up liquid will be appropriate. Thoroughly rinse the bottle until the water runs clear and clean before offering it to a chinchilla.

Discard and replace the sand in the dust bath.

To ensure no loose hair is built up around the cage due to shedding (see chapter on Shedding), it is advisable to brush down the inside of the cage focusing on the joins of shelves, corners and especially the floor. This will ensure the cage is well ventilated and free from elements such as dust, which can cause irritation to the chinchilla's eyes and nose.

Twice Yearly

Give the cage a complete "spring-clean".

Take out all toys and accessories so the cage is completely empty before disinfecting both the inside and outside, making sure it is rinsed well with water before drying.

All washable accessories should be sterilized including the dust bath and completely dried before returning them into the cage.

Any non-washable toys should be disregarded and replaced.

Keeping the cage clean will promote good health in your chinchilla

Sampson - Standard Grey, Male Kit, 1 week old.

BASIC NECESSATIES

There are some basic necessities your chinchilla will need in order to survive and stay healthy:

1) **Water Bottle** - Fresh water daily will help prevent constipation and promote good health. The bottle should be hung on the outside of the cage to prevent chewing and leakages. A bowl will not be adequate for chinchillas, as the water will either be spilt or soiled with urine, droppings or food.

2) **Food Bowl** - There are various types of food bowls available, either clipping on the outside of the cage funnelling into a dish on the inside or a bowl that clips on the inside of the cage. A heavy ceramic bowl that can not be tipped over can also be used.

Chinchillas do not like to eat their food sitting on the floor which explains their un-table like manners when you see them sitting on the rim of their bowl, therefore have something solid nearby which they can stand on whilst eating.

Sweetie eating from food bowl.

3) **Hay Rack** - Pet shops sell various hayracks that can clip inside the cage or alternatively you can use a heavy ceramic bowl. Most 'bought' chinchilla cages include a hayrack made out of the galvanised mesh so the hay can poke through for easy consumption by a chinchilla. Chinchillas will also be content with the hay left on a shelf but you will need to ensure it is changed daily to prevent contamination from urine.

It is also possible to now purchase hay houses in various shapes and sizes; these are

Hay rack with hooks to attach to the cage.

long pieces of hay and straw wrapped around wires. If you decide to use these, caution should be taken when the hay is getting low that no sharp ends of the wire is exposed as this could seriously harm your pet. Hay cubes can also be purchased for those owners and chinchillas who are sensitive to dust, these generally come in alfalfa form.

4) **Pumice Stone** - Your chinchilla's teeth will need constant filing, a pumice stone is excellent for this purpose and can be purchased from most pet shops.

5) **House** - Your chinchilla will need a place to rest and hide and anything placed inside your chinchilla cage will eventually get eaten. The

In built hayrack.

healthiest type of house is one that is made out of untreated natural pine.

You can purchase houses from pet shops but these are generally made up of plywood, which can be extremely dangerous to

Chinchilla House.

a chinchilla if fully consumed. The plywood is made out of pieces of wood and glue, which can splinter; alternatively a cardboard box is an excellent idea.

6) **Dust-Bath** - You can purchase a dust-bath from your local pet shop, or alternatively you can use any large container available as long as it is big enough for the chinchilla to roll about in. Large family size sweet tins are excellent and have high sides to prevent the dust from spilling out as it is kicked around.

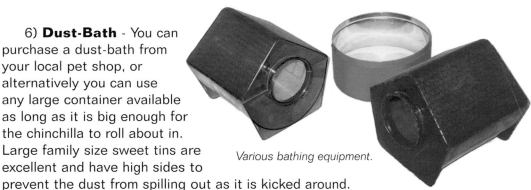

Various bathing equipment.

New on the market are dust houses, these are made of plastic and have a roof, which again are excellent to prevent dust spillage. Your chinchillas will need separate baths to stop any present infections spreading although saying this, it is quite hard to manage as mine likc to jump into one anothers bath when the other is finished just to check it out!

Basic Necessities; House, Hay, Water, Pellets, Pumice Stone & Sand Bath.

ADDITIONAL ASSESORIES/TOYS

Your chinchilla will be extremely inquisitive therefore you will need to put accessories in their cage to encourage curiosity. It is a good idea when cleaning the cage that you rearrange their playthings, they will love this and prevent them becoming bored.

Tree branches are excellent to put in a cage, the bark will be consumed leaving the branches for the chinchillas to play and jump on. Ensure they are firmly placed in a cage, wedging them between wires and that they are made of wood that is healthy to the chinchilla's digestive tract.

Safe branches to use are apple, pear, willow, and hazelnut. You should only use with caution: juniper, birch, aspen, oak and ash-tree.

Never use: any branches from citrus trees, grapefruit, cherry or wild cherry, cedar, walnut, redwood and fresh pine branches. Fresh pine branches can contain pitch - a dark sticky resin derived from the sap of pine trees.

Ladders - Are a great way of getting to different levels. The ladder should preferably have a solid back to it so the chinchilla cannot slip through the holes; therefore, you may need to make your own as these are not readily available in

Additional Accessories.

Wooden toys and apple tree branch.

pet shops. If you do purchase one without a back to it, ensure the length between the steps is big enough so if your chinchilla does fall it will not get stuck between the rails and break any bones.

Cardboard Boxes - Are excellent as an alternative home if you cut a big hole in the side for them to get into. Cardboard boxes will not last long as your chinchilla home, as it will be eaten and destroyed quite quickly by your pet, although they will provide them with hours of fun. Ensure there is not much print on the side of the box as this can be toxic to a chinchilla.

Toilet Rolls or Carpet Rolls - It is very amusing to watch your chinchilla bounce around with these in their mouth. Saying this they should be used with caution on kits as my female chinchilla once got her head stuck in the toilet roll and was unable to get it off! Luckily she did not panic too much and I got there just in time, therefore it is wise to rip the roll first before giving it to kits.

Sweetie playing with a cardboard roll.

Plastic Tubes - Should be purchased from your pet shop, ones in builders' merchants can contain toxins that can be harmful to a chinchilla. Tubes increase a chinchillas natural behaviour of burrowing and can be connected together to make a wonderful adventure route,

your pet may even choose these to sleep in.

Carpet - Chinchillas love to eat carpet, anyone that lets their pet run free will agree! They will toss the piece about the cage, lie on it and generally demolish it. Ensure it has a woven back as the foam backing can contain elements that are unsafe to a chinchilla's digestive tract.

Bird Accessories - Some bird accessories are perfect to entertain your chinchilla. The best type are the

Joey- Hetero Beige, Male playing in his plastic tube.

dangly creations made of pinewood with a bell at the end that you can hang within the cage. They love to hear the jingling of the bell but ensure the bells are fully intact before giving it to your chinchilla. Never buy a bird swing or ladder for them as they will try and jump on it and hurt themselves.

Wooden Stacks - These are relatively new to the chinchilla range but are fantastic. They are small branches covered with bark, interlocked with wire that can be bent in different directions. They can be made into houses, ladders or used as a hideaway. Your chinchilla will adore them and they are perfectly safe for their health.

Wooden stacks made into tunnels and bridges.

Wooden Blocks - Various wooden blocks can be purchased for your chinchilla to chew on. Some come with their bark still on which is excellent nutrition, whilst others are made from pine that has been stained various colours. These can either be left loose around the cage or a hole drilled through them so they can be attached around the cage to cause diversity.

Dried Cactus Chew Blocks.

Large Pebbles - My chinchillas love these. A chinchilla can use the stone to file their teeth, move them about or lie on them when the weather gets hot. I have seen one chinchilla gnaw down a large pebble to almost nothing!

Cheeky on large pebble.

10 PROMISES TO MY CHINCHILLA

1) I promise to never cause you any intentional harm.
2) I promise to never desert you.
3) I promise to never mistreat you.
4) I promise to provide the best possible care during your entire lifetime.
5) I promise to contact a qualified vet immediately at first signs of illness.
6) I promise to give and show you patience at all times.
7) I promise to never chase or scare you.
8) I promise to never punish you.
9) I promise to never cause you any undue stress or mishandling.
10) I promise to never ignore you.

Mark - Hetero Ebony, Male, 2 days old.

BRINGING YOUR PET HOME

The pet shop should place your new chinchilla in a dark cardboard box with holes in the side, this is a good form of transport for a short journey as it is dark and increases security. If you have some way to travel home it is a good idea to take a small carrier with you that is well ventilated as chinchillas do not travel well and can easily become over-heated and die!

It is wise to ask the pet shop what time of day they feed the chinchilla and which type of pellets they have been using - ask for a small supply to take with you.

Chinchillas do not like abrupt changes with their diet. Their digestive tracts are very sensitive therefore it is a good idea to mix some of their old pellets with the new ones you have bought and gradually over a 2 week period fade out the old type.

Once you have the chinchilla home, the best idea is to place it in its new cage, give him/her a treat and leave it alone for a while.

The new chinchilla will be acting quite nervous especially if it has just been taken from its mother and does not know any other type of environment. Moving to a new environment and owner is extremely stressful to a chinchilla and can even cause death if not done correctly.

Ensure the room is quiet, if it is daytime the chinchilla will most probably explore for a while then find somewhere to sleep.

For the first day or two it is best to refrain from holding your chinchilla, as they need time to trust you. Holding a chinchilla too soon will end up with you covered in their fur as this is their defence mechanism against being caught and the process will only take longer.

When approaching the cage, move slowly, talking quietly and calmly to your new friend, never hover over the cage causing a shadow, this will terrify them. It helps if you sit near the cage and talk to him/her quietly. At first the chinchilla will most probably start running all over the place

Chinchillas love a treat! This little furball is munching on an almond. Furby – Black Velvet, Male.

frantically, not knowing what to do but within time it will settle down. Curiosity usually wins them over and slowly they begin to approach the side where you are sitting.

When they approach, you can give them a tiny treat (not if they are young though!) and praise them calmly. Any sudden movements will scare your chinchilla into a dark corner so it is advisable when you change their food bowl and water that you do so very slowly.

Chinchillas thrive on routine, especially when it comes to times of eating. They have been known to completely stress out if their dinner is moved to another time of the day. Any changes should be made slowly.

At first try to keep with the routine that they have been used to either in the pet shop or with the breeder and slowly make the changes to suit your lifestyle.

DIET & FEEDING

Chinchillas are primarily herbivores (plant eaters), in the wild they would consume tree bark, grasses, seed, fruit, grains and herbs, but in captivity their main diet is water, pellets and hay.

Some owners feed their chinchillas in the morning and evening but it is up to you when you want to feed yours.

Their diet should be made up of 16-20% protein, 4% fat, 18% fibre, 6% minerals and 10% moisture/trace elements

Water - Chinchilla's have the ability to retain water in their fur and tails and do not seem to drink that much. Saying this, it is essential and should be provided fresh on a daily basis. It is best to boil tap water and allow it to cool before providing it to your chinchilla. Adult chinchillas can consume anything between 15-40mls a day.

Pellets - A fully grown chinchilla will eat up to 2 tablespoons of pellets a day (approximately 20 grams), therefore never give them too much as it will be wasted.

Mature chinchillas will generally not over eat, but this cannot be said for kits. Many have been known to die from being over fed at an early age, so it is essential that you only feed the kit half the daily recommendation (i.e. 1-tablespoon). Very slowly increase the amount each day until maturity (8 months).

Pellets do not keep indefinitely therefore it is best to store them in a refrigerator and not buy a big bulk (sold in bags from 2lb-50lbs (1-22kilos).

Bowl of chinchilla pellets.

Pellets consist of hulled oats, molasses, soybean, wheat, alfalfa, vitamins and minerals and generally the nutrients will diminish after 3 months. For optimum health, disregard old supplies and buy new.

You should only use pellets that have been made for chinchillas.

Rabbit or Guinea Pig pellets should never under any circumstance be given as they include hormones that can be fatal to the chinchilla and make them fat. Females have also been known to have difficulty conceiving when eating rabbit pellets.

Good quality pellets should hold nutritional values of 16-20% protein, 18% fibre and no more than 5% fat.

Hay - A constant supply of hay is essential to a chinchilla's health and teeth just as much as pellets. Hay should be kept crisp and dry at all times within the cage and any damp, wet or mouldy hay should be disregarded, as this will induce diarrhoea or other health issues.

Standard meadow hay is typically 7% protein and 33% fibre, therefore high in fibre with a low protein content and should be present within the diet at all times.

If you find that loose hay is inappropriate, you can now purchase either hay cubes or a hay house of various sizes. Houses are made up of long pieces of hay wrapped around wires. If you decide to use these, caution should be taken when the hay is getting low that no sharp ends of the wire is exposed as this could seriously harm your pet.

Alfalfa hay can also be given but not as a permanent substitute for standard hay as it is made up of high fibre as well as a high

Meadow Hay, suitable for chinchillas.

proportion of protein. Alfalfa nutritional qualities vary from: 18% protein and 29% fibre but some can have a higher protein content. Alfalfa is safe to give as a treat on a regular basis and is excellent in helping the chinchilla file his/her teeth.

Treats - Chinchillas LOVE treats but should only be given by hand as mixed into food will inevitably cause a chinchilla to pick out the tasty treats and leave their pellets.

Giving treats by hand will also help your chinchilla to trust and bond with you. Although sunflower seeds can be given, their amount should be limited; not only high in fat they can also cause a deficiency in calcium levels.

There are only certain types of treats that are suitable for the chinchilla's sensitive digestive tract and even these must be given in moderation.

½ grape, untreated natural rolled oats, 1 dried thistle, 1 rosehip, 2 raisins, thin slice of apple, kiwi, pear or plum, 1 fresh/dried cranberry, blueberry or redberry, small piece of toast crust, 2 sunflower seeds, dandelion leaves and roots (picked from your own untreated garden, soak in salted water, then rinse well), bitesize shreaded wheat.

Apple rings, cranberries, porridge oats, red berries, rose hips, sultanas and sunflower seeds.

0-3 months - No treats (this can kill them!)
3-8 months - ½ teaspoon
8 months + - 1 teaspoon

REMEMBER: These are treats! A chinchilla would not normally find such luxuries in the wild therefore they are not built to digest such rich foods. Only give in moderation and times of training, as overdose will cause gastric problems such as diarrhoea, entherisis, fattening of the heart and early death.

Supplements - Generally if you are providing good quality, fresh pellets and hay to your chinchilla there should be no need to add supplements.

Occasionally during a chinchilla's lifetime they may be in need of extra supplementation, if for any reason you feel you would like to add supplements, you must remember to do so gradually and also observe the chinchilla to check for no harmful side effects.

Vitamin C - Supplements have been looked into and it is suggested that an increase in this vitamin can reduce the chances of your chinchilla having gum or teeth problems.

Missy – White Mosaic, Female.

50mg chewable Children's Vitamin C tablet would be sufficient but you must ensure it has no added iron or Vitamin A. You can also introduce Vitamin C into the diet by providing fresh berries (see treats listed above) and kiwi.

Calcium - In the form of a Tums tablet is another supplement that can be added to your chinchillas diet. It is recommended that both pregnant chinchillas and kits under one year should receive an extra helping of calcium to aid healthy bones and dental growth (always check with your vet first and only ever give a kit half of the recommended dosage). If a chinchilla is eating good quality hay, it should not need extra calcium.

Teeth, which are white in colour, are severely lacking calcium and any deficiencies in this mineral can lead to seizures and brain damage.

Vionate Powder - For exotic pets is a combination of vitamins and minerals that can be bought from the larger pet stores and sprinkled over the top of pellets.

Salt Spools - Can also be added and are readily available from larger pet shops.

Jasper – Standard Grey, Male.

Probiotic Powder - Also known as Avipro Plus obtained from a vet contains live bacteria to help regulate the chinchillas gut. This can be given daily within the water.

It is debatable whether chinchillas need supplementation, therefore if you are unsure, then refrain from doing so or check with your vet first. You would not want to kill your pet whilst trying to help him! Never offer supplements to a kit unless on the agreement of a qualified vet.

TAMING A CHINCHILLA

After a few days (usually 4-10 days) when the chinchilla is happily sitting near you calmly in the cage, he is ready to meet your hands again. Remember at this stage the only memory they have of your hands is when you were examining them in a shop or putting them into a new environment, both of which caused them a lot of stress.

You should not allow your new chinchilla outside of his/her cage until they have learnt to trust you and have bonded with you. If a chinchilla is loose outside their cage they will be even harder to catch and the catching process will cause them to loose any trust built up with you.

You should start by opening the cage door slowly and placing your hand inside offering the chinchilla a treat. The chinchilla will eventually come up to your hand and within time jump on it and begin to explore. It is a good idea to move a treat up your arm; this will encourage the chinchilla to climb further on you thereby obtaining more trust.

When both you and the chinchilla are relaxed with this stage you can move onto placing a hand over them in preparation to picking them up. This is best done whilst they are eating their treat, it will take time (maybe months) but patience is the name of the game.

Eventually when the chinchilla is used to this process, pick him/her up by placing one hand underneath and one on top and bring it closely to your chest for security. The chinchilla will be extremely appreciative of a treat at this stage which will help for repeated behaviour.

Please remember that unless a chinchilla is trained from an early age it will probably never like you holding it so try and get him/her used to this early on.

Place your hand inside the cage and offer the chinchilla a treat (Knuffel – Grey Standard, Male).

If a chinchilla really does not like to be handled, please do not force them otherwise it will undo any trust or bonding that you have already achieved. They have individual personalities and not all chinchillas like to be handled.

PLAYING WITH A CHINCHILLA

I cannot stress enough how important play is to a chinchilla especially if there is only one. It is a time of learning, trusting and bonding and should be done at a regular time each and every night and ended with a treat.

Play must be completely supervised and should be done outside of the cage. You must ensure that the area is completely 'chinchilla proof' as they love to chew and find escape routes.

Anything that is dangerous if eaten should be removed, windows securely shut, electrical cords withdrawn from their sockets, doors closed and any other pets removed.

The scene should be quiet where the only voices heard are of you and your pet. Never run about, jump or move quickly as this will frighten your chinchilla back into retreat.

Chinchillas love to run, jump, hide, nibble and explore. When in full swing of contentment they can be seen jumping around off the floor on all fours, it is quite funny and you will cherish the moment!

You can provide them with toys such as cardboard hiding boxes, carpet-roll tubes, leather boots/shoes, plastic tubes, stones/rocks etc.

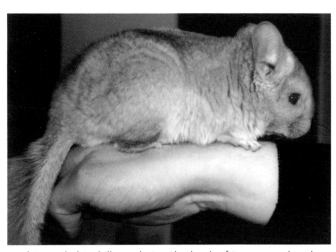

A tamed chinchilla exploring the back of its owners hand.

During play, chinchillas display their own characteristics just like ourselves, one may love to sit and be stroked around the ears and under the chin, whereas another may be content just running around exploring.

They will teach you their version of 'hide 'n' seek' and 'it!' and will be completely happy to jump all over you. They will nibble your toes, ears, eyebrows and eyelashes. My female even gives me a haircut if I let her, although I must admit it is not very even! (Having one chinchilla on your head fishing through your hair whilst the other is on the tips of your toes nibbling your feet is really quite something).

Their intelligence has been compared to that of the squirrel and when repeated will learn the words, *bath, come here, no, their name, treat, good boy/girl etc.*

They can also learn certain tricks such as begging, sitting up, jumping and coming when called if taught slowly followed by a favourite treat. Please do not expect too much though as they can be extremely funny just as they are.

Never let a chinchilla play outside for various reasons: it could escape, another animal may attack it, if sunny - it may overheat needless to say that the sudden changes in climate and temperature are not good for a chinchillas health.

EXERCISING A CHINCHILLA

It is important to the chinchilla's health and well being that he should be allowed time out of the cage, by doing so you will be providing extra space to run, exercising the heart and respiratory system.

If it is impossible for a chinchilla to come out of its cage then it is wise to purchase a chinchilla wheel (see chapter on Chinchilla Wheel) to provide the exercise that he needs.

A chinchilla weighs between 14-21ozs (400-600 grams) and anything other than this is unhealthy and will be putting undue stress on their systems potentially causing harm and death.

Exercise should be daily for a minimum of one hour and can come in the form of play or general exercise.

Violet male – 6 months old running on his spinning wheel (patent number 6,578,526).

You can now purchase exercise balls which open up for a chinchilla to be placed inside then securely closed before the chinchilla is allowed to run around the room freely.

Using such balls should be done in small doses of no longer than 15 minutes at a time as the temperature within the ball becomes hot from the chinchillas bodyheat and combined with exercise can cause the chinchilla to overheat (see Health Guide - Heat Stroke).

It is best to give the chinchilla a secure area within a room which can be explored freely (whilst being supervised). There is no time limit on this type of exercise, as the chinchilla will have good air ventilation.

Ensure all doors and windows are closed and harmful objects are removed before allowing your chinchilla to run freely, remember they will chew anything!

EXERCISE WHEELS

If time out of the cage is very limited it is a good idea to purchase an exercise wheel to help your chinchillas get the daily exercise they need. A wheel can be an invaluable accessory to help aid your chinchillas health and fitness regime and also relieve boredom or behaviour problems.

Not all chinchillas will like an exercise wheel so do not be disappointed if you do get one and it just sits in the cage collecting dust!

Care must be taken when buying a wheel, as some can be seriously dangerous to a clumsy chinchilla either ripping their feet off or getting their head jammed in the spokes, therefore you should only purchase a wheel if it meets specific requirements.

When a chinchilla stretches they average approximately 12"-14" (30cm x 35cm) therefore an exercise wheel must be of this diameter, preferably slightly bigger if no spinal damage is to occur. You must ensure the running surface is between 4½"-5" (11cm x 13cm) wide to prevent the chinchilla from falling off.

There must be no spokes running across the middle of the wheel to potentially crush any limbs or head as it is turning and must be made of a solid running surface to ensure no trapped toes.

Some people use mesh running surfaces of ¼" x ¼" (6mm x 6mm) successfully but it is better to be safe than sorry as these little fluff balls run at great speeds. Catching a toe or finger is easy and can even be missed by the owner! If you are unsure of which to choose then purchase a solid running base.

Wheels that clip on the side of the cage securely are the best forms, this way when they jump onto the running track it will be sturdy enough to not fall over and cause any harm.

The position of the wheel is equally important as at first chinchillas will not know what it is and will generally jump on top of it and start running at full speed only to be catapulted across the cage potentially causing broken limbs and concussion!

It is wise to place the wheel close to the floor so chinchillas cannot get trapped under it. Place a shelf above the wheel to stop any dare devils from jumping on top (even worse another chinchilla jumping on top whilst one is in/on the wheel...a definite set up for potential injury!).

When a chinchilla has worked out how the wheel works they will either like it and be grateful to have something to waste away many hours of boredom or it will be gratefully received as a resting place. Either way a properly manufactured chinchilla wheel can be an excellent accessory to any chinchilla cage.

CATCHING A CHINCHILLA

Catching an escaped chinchilla is quite an ordeal, not only for the owner but more so for the chinchilla. Generally if a chinchilla is left to its own devises it will return to its cage eventually but if you need to catch the escapee there are a couple of methods you could try.

L-R: Timmy, Storm (Father & Son, both Black Velvets), Smokey & Dot (Mother & Daughter, both Standard Grey).

Teaching the chinchilla its name may help it to come back to you willingly but if a chinchilla is resistant the best thing to do is to try and call it back by offering it a treat or its dust bath. Generally these things will work with a bit of patience but if you have a determined chinchilla on your hands who is happy to give you the run around then the first rule is to never ever chase it!

Chasing a chinchilla will cause it to do three things, hide, go into shock at this great shadow towering over it trying to grab it or it will completely exhaust the chinchilla causing it to over heat, stress and potentially die.

If the treats or dust bath do not work then you can use a sheet or towel to gently throw over the chinchilla who will then freeze long enough for you to pick it up and place it back in its cage.

If you grab at a chinchilla all you will get is a handful of fur as it will use one of its defence mechanisms and release its fur whilst it runs off underneath!

If the chinchilla is in hiding, then you will need to be patient and coax it out of its hole with treats or a bath, sit away from the area and let the chinchilla come out before quickly picking it up and placing it back into its cage.

Remember an escaped chinchilla is a stressed out chinchilla!

Ensure all areas of freedom are fully secured and should your chinchilla ever escape, never chase it, it will only run from you not to you! Patience is the name of this game and patience and gentle coaxing is the only answer in catching an escapee...GOOD LUCK!

LOOKING AFTER & CARING FOR A CHINCHILLA

Coming from the harsh weathers of the Andes have made this small creature tough and hardy. Providing they are given the correct type of care in captivity there is no reason why they should not live as long as they would if in the wild.

However, there are times when health problems occur (see Health Guide Section) but if you follow the fundamentals of looking after a chinchilla the chances of them becoming unwell will be limited.

EXAMINE your pet on a regular basis, perhaps when you have picked him up would be

D'Artagnan – Black Velvet, Male.

a good time and would not cause any further stress. By doing this you will notice any differences in health sooner which can be treated in its early stages.

CHECK its ears, nose, mouth, anus, sexual organs and around the eyes. The eyes and faeces are the first indicators that there is a health problem and at first signs you should contact a qualified veterinary surgeon that has experience of treating chinchillas.

FRESH food and water should be given daily and any leftovers or loose, damp hay discarded.

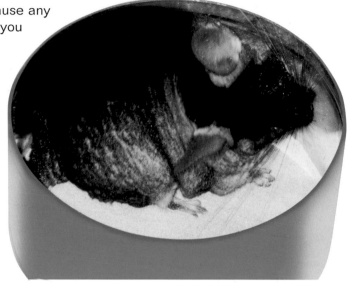

Sweetie (Black Velvet, Female) taking a sand bath.

CLEAN and check the cage regularly for sharp objects or fungus formation. Ensure it is well ventilated at all times. A clean cage will encourage good grooming in your chinchilla and promote good health.

DUSTBATHS should be given regularly. It is debatable how often to give a bath as too often can cause a chinchilla to dry out, become flaky and itchy. On the other hand too few baths will cause your chinchilla to become oily and messy looking.

Word of warning here - chinchilla's are known to not ever bath again if they have been left too long without one. Once out of the habit, they will not get back into a bath under any circumstances, therefore ensure your chinchilla has a bath at least once a week.

FREEDOM to run freely on a regular basis. If this is not possible then do not buy a chinchilla. If they are kept in the cages for long periods they will deteriorate and suffer ill health.

DON'T NEGLECT or ignore your chinchilla, it thrives on love, company, attention and is very sensitive. Chinchillas have been known to become so stressed out if there owner has gone on holiday that they have shed all their fur, by the time the owner has got back their chinchillas were bald!

ADHERE to the chapter on '10 Promises to My Chinchilla'.

TRAVELLING WITH A CHINCHILLA

Chinchillas do not travel well therefore wherever possible it is always best to leave them at home with a reliable and knowledgeable baby sitter.

There are two methods available for transporting your chinchillas and for short journeys one way is securely in a towel.

Place a towel on your lap with the chinchilla on top and wrap the towel around the chinchilla ensuring all areas of the body are securely within the towel except its head. You must go very careful with this method if your chinchilla is not to escape from the towel when out in the open, if you are nervous or unsure I would recommend you use a well-ventilated box or buy a travelling cage.

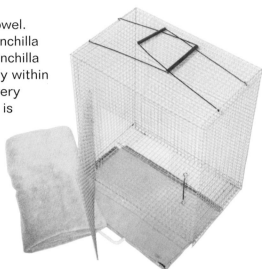

Travel Cage and Towel used for chinchilla transportation.

I would never recommend a towel or ventilated box for long journeys as your pet will be guaranteed heat-stroke (see Health Guide) and potentially die. The best method of transport for long journeys is a travel cage accompanied by basic necessities such as water, pellets and a waste tray.

The cage should contain the minimum of necessities and the odd toy to prevent flying injuries whilst in transport and never place the cage on the floor of transport where it gets hotter. Windows should be kept open at all times for general ventilation and a chinchilla never left unattended in the car.

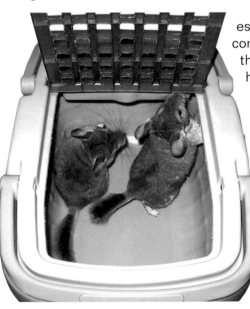

Another type of travelling cage for short journeys, a cat box can also be used.

A cage must be secure with no forms of escape and it is wise if travelling in warm conditions, to include some frozen ice packs in the cage to prevent the chinchilla from over heating.

During the journey wherever possible, the chinchillas should be kept quiet and calm to prevent shock and ensure survival of the ordeal.

When the destination is reached they should be placed back into the original home and given a treat before being left to calm down and return to normal.

Only travel with a chinchilla if it is absolutely necessary, not many survive the trauma of a long distance trek (remember Chapman's journey?) therefore careful planning and care must be adhered to.

SHEDDING

Every three months a chinchilla will shed its fur. This sounds more alarming than it actually is as the fur comes out gradually from the neck and moves down over the whole body. You can help it along by grooming your chinchilla but it is not necessary.

The shedding period usually lasts approximately 2 weeks; therefore at these times it is imperative that you collect any loose hair to prevent it flying around the cage causing eye irritations.

You may notice a distinct line running across the body called a 'priming line', this distinguishes the old growth from the new. A chinchilla is considered at its prime (best coat condition) when the line has reached its tail.

GROOMING A CHINCHILLA

Combing a chinchilla is not really necessary especially if they are given regular dust baths. Dust - I hear you say? Yes, I did mean a 'dust' bath, as they do not bathe in water and would not appreciate being given one!

Their bath should be at least 2" (5 cm) deep of dust similar to the volcanic ash found in the Andes.

Use a tin big enough for a chinchilla to have a good roll about in and allow him/her to roll about freely in the dust for 5-10 minutes preferably in the morning. If left in for too long, your chinchilla will begin to use it as a toilet!

After a night of activities a bath in the morning before bed will be a luxury to a chinchilla, although saying this if the morning does not fit into your routine, then an evening bath is still appreciated by a chinchilla.

Only dust made especially for chinchillas should be used and can be found in most pet shops. Try different brands to find which suits your chinchilla the best.

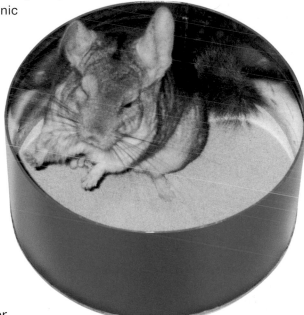

Ensure the container is big enough for a chinchilla to roll about in.

If you wish to comb your chinchilla (although it really is not necessary) you will have better results if he/she is happy to be handled and fussed over, if not your chinchilla will not appreciate the intrusion and may begin to lack trust in you and become scared.

Combing a chinchilla should be done very carefully and never harshly. It is best to comb a chinchilla before its bath to help separate the fur so the dust can easily clean the skin

Steady your chinchilla over a towel on your lap, either by holding him/her by the base of the tail (the part that's near the body not the tip!) or place a hand in front of the chest and wait until the chinchilla has calmed.

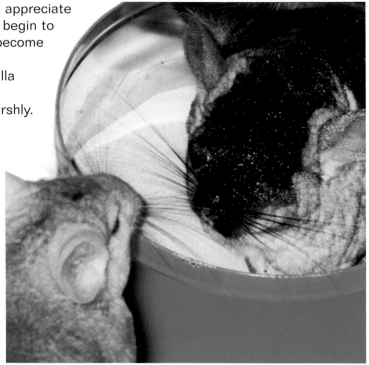

Chinchillas love to share one another's bath.

Starting at the rear with a wide toothed comb, separate and comb small sections only, be careful so you do not accidentally scratch the animals skin and cause inflammation. Continue in small sections working up the back and sides until you have reached the neck.

You can comb a chinchilla's belly but it is a lot more difficult as they are not too keen on lying on their backs and staying still for long! If you choose to comb the stomach do so in small sections at a time to prevent pulling the hair and hurting your pet.

You can repeat the whole process afterwards with a fine toothed comb to further loosen hair but only do this if the chinchilla is really enjoying it.

BREEDING CHINCHILLAS

Never consider breeding chinchillas if you are unsure of what you are doing as they need a lot of care and attention. When you take away the laws of nature, the knowledge and responsibility of the breeder is of great importance if a healthy pregnancy is to take place.

You must understand fully the genetics of a chinchilla and not manipulate or change any of the breeding techniques of Mother Nature to achieve a certain feature such as colour, unless you are completely qualified.

In some cases breeding for this purpose can be problematic to both the mother and the newborn. Devastating defects in the kit such as malocclusion can occur, which is a defect between the upper and lower teeth on contact when the jaw is closed. Malocclusion is fatal to a chinchilla as they will not be able to feed themselves and will die.

You should also be aware that there is a reduced chance of conception if you breed certain coloured chinchillas together because of genetics, therefore you will need to ensure that the parents and grandparents of your chinchilla are also checked out. This is imperative and any uncertainties should be left to the experienced breeder!

You must also remember that you will need to find good homes for your chinchilla's babies and you will need to ensure if these babies are to have babies, that their potential owner is as thorough as you in finding their babies new homes and so on... This responsibility should not be taken lightly if no harm is to come of your chinchilla's kits.

Leo – Dark Tan, Male – 1 year old.

CHINCHILLA GENETICS

To discuss genetics my terminology and assessment is by no means as comprehensive as a scientific appraisal or explanation and is only a basic overview that should be remembered. This chapter will help an inexperienced chinchilla owner understand the basic reasons why we say that particular colour mutations should not be bred together and the implications.

To begin to understand chinchilla genetics you must first become familiar with two main terms:

Homozygous (the same) - This means that the chinchilla has two genes (alleles) of the same type. The chinchilla will possess either 2 dominant genes know as 'AA' or 2 recessive genes known as 'aa'.

Heterozygous (different) - this means that the chinchilla has two genes (alleles) different to one another known as 'Aa' (a dominant gene (A) and a recessive gene (a)).

A recessive gene will be weaker in reproduction than the more dominant gene, for example a white mosaic has a dominant gene of white (A) and a recessive gene of grey (a) therefore it will be prominently more white with grey markings. The same applies for other characteristics of the stronger gene, for example, eye colour, fur density, temperament size etc. all these will be mainly influenced by the dominant gene.

Houdini – TOV Beige, Male.

For the purpose of this book I will focus only on the genetic gene for fur colour, as this seems to cause the most interest.

Different colour mutations have derived from the original wild Standard Grey chinchilla that possess 2 recessive 'grey influenced colour' genes.

There are 3 colour mutations who's genes are more superior to the Standard Grey's, these being White, Beige and Black Velvet (TOV or Touch of Velvet).

The genes of these colour mutations will be prominently more influential than the recessive genes of the Standard Grey and can also be referred to as the 'Dominant Mutation Colours'.

There are also 3 colour mutations whose genes to influence colour are weaker than the Standard Grey, these being Ebony (Charcoal), Sapphire and Violet. They are more commonly referred to as the 'Recessive Mutation Colours'.

If a Recessive Mutation Colour is to be noticeable in the fur, then one of the breeding chinchillas must be of that particular Recessive Colour Mutation and fall into the category - Homozygous Dominant (i.e. both genes the same and dominant (AA)). If the Recessive Colour Mutation carries the Heterozygous gene then the chinchilla will be a carrier.

EXAMPLE; Shows a Recessive Mutation Colour (Violet) in the Homozygous Dominant form (AA) versus a Dominant Mutation Colour (White) in the Heterozygous form (Aa)

	Homozygous Violet Dominant gene (A)	Homozygous Violet Dominant gene (A)
Heterozygous White Dominant gene (A)	White-Violet Carrier	White-Violet Carrier
Heterozygous White Recessive gene (a)	White-Violet	White-Violet

In this example white is the Dominant Colour Mutation, therefore, when it is combined with the Recessive Colour Mutation of Violet, chinchillas will result in being white and carry the Violet gene (commonly known as White/Violet carriers). Alternatively when the Dominant Colour Mutation of White falls into the Recessive gene category (a) and meets with a Dominant Violet gene (A), this combination will result in a White Violet. The above example produces 50% White chinchillas who will carry the Violet gene and 50% White chinchillas with visible Violet in the fur.

It should be remembered that breeding for colour should be left up to the experts as it holds a complex responsibility regarding breeding particular colour mutations together.

There is much discussion about the pregnancy complications in breeding certain colour mutations together, these being:

White	-	White
Black velvet	-	Black Velvet (or any TOV to another TOV, i.e. TOV Violet, TOV White, Brown Velvet etc.)

It is not possible for the above colour mutations to exist in the Homozygous form and therefore should never be attempted. For the purposes of genetic breeding, 'white' will mean anything from pure white to splashes of white within the fur; even these should not be bred together, the same will apply to black and any TOV!

For an example, if a white egg meets with a white sperm (even if it is not a dominant gene and is only slightly seen on the coat) 25% less offspring will be produced. Therefore breeding these colour combinations together, should be avoided.

EXAMPLE 2:
In the event that conception is successful, it is known that 25% of the eggs would not develop, 25% would be Standard in colour and the remaining 50% will be Heterozygous, (identical to their parents).

	Heterozygous White Dominant gene (A)	Heterozygous White Recessive gene (a)
Heterozygous White Dominant gene (A)	Fatality	Heterozygous White (Aa)
Heterozygous White Recessive gene (a)	Heterozygous White (Aa)	Standard Grey (aa)

Again this is only a very basic explanation of genetics that influence colour and factors to look out for. For a more comprehensive understanding, further research should be undertaken and advice sought from a reputable source.

If you are ever unsure if it is safe to breed a particular colour combination then do not attempt to do so before seeking qualified help.

CREATING COLOURS

Certain factors should also be considered when breeding for colour such as: standards of health, the quality of fur, temperament, size and behaviour, all these features can be affected when mixing certain colour mutations together.

The information provided in these chapters is by no means comprehensive and is intended to provide only brief guidelines on how colours are achieved.

Punnet Squares are commonly used to calculate the potential of achieving a particular colour.

The genes of one parent are shown along the top and the genes of the other shown down the left-hand side. The 4 meeting squares then indicate the predictions of that particular match.

	A	A
A	AA	AA
a	Aa	Aa

EXAMPLE 1
Chin 1 Standard Grey (aa) - Chin 2 Standard Grey (aa)

	Standard Grey Recessive gene (a)	Standard Grey Recessive gene (a)
Standard Grey Recessive gene (a)	Standard Grey (aa)	Standard Grey (aa)
Standard Grey Recessive gene (a)	Standard Grey (aa)	Standard Grey (aa)

100% of the offspring of this combination will be Standard Grey with Homozygous Recessive genes (aa)

EXAMPLE 2
Both Chinchillas Heterozygous Beige (A-Dominant a-Recessive genes)

	Beige Dominant gene (A)	Beige Recessive gene (a)
Beige Dominant gene (A)	Beige (AA)	Beige (Aa)
Beige Recessive gene (a)	Beige (Aa)	Standard (aa)

The combination above shows a production of 50% Heterozygous Beige (Aa), 25% Homozygous Beige (AA) and 25% Standard Grey (aa). Standard Grey is produced as the Recessive gene (a) in a Heterozygous Beige is grey influenced.

EXAMPLE 3
Chin 1 Homozygous Ebony Dominant (AA)
Chin 2 Standard (aa)

	Homozygous Ebony Dominant (A)	Homozygous Ebony Dominant (A)
Recessive Standard Grey (a)	Ebony (Aa)	Ebony (Aa)
Recessive Standard Grey (a)	Ebony (Aa)	Ebony (Aa)

As Ebony is a Dominant Colour Mutation over Standard Grey this combination will result in 100% Ebony kits with Heterozygous genes (Aa), also known as Hetero Ebony.

EXAMPLE 4
Chin 1 Black Velvet (Aa)
Chin 2 Hetero Beige (Aa)

	Black Velvet Dominant Gene (A)	Black Velvet Recessive Gene (a)
Beige Dominant Gene (A)	Black/Beige (AA) *Brown Velvet*	Beige/Standard (Aa) *Hetero Beige*
Beige Recessive Gene (a)	Black/Standard (Aa) *Black Velvet*	Standard/Standard (aa) *Grey Standard*

The above combination would result in 25% Standard Grey, 25% Hetero Beige, 25% Black Velvet, 25% TOV Beige (Brown Velvet).

These are just some basic examples of how to calculate a potential colour mutation outcome, more results can be found under the Chinchilla Colouring chapter.

Chinchillas, which feel secure and happy, will generally produce healthy offspring automatically without any interference or help from us.

If you want your pets to have babies just follow a few simple rules and you should witness the birth of healthy, happy kits:

1) Ensure you trace white, black and TOV genetics back by 2 generations.
2) Ensure the cage position is in a quiet and secure environment.
3) Provide a pregnant mother the correct nutrients and care she needs.
4) Follow the guidelines in the Mating Chinchillas chapter.
5) Be there to witness the birth just in case you are needed.

INTRODUCING CHINCHILLA'S

Unless chinchillas are together from birth they will need to be introduced to each other. It is extremely important that this stage is not rushed if a chinchilla is to survive. There are no guarantees that two chinchillas will get along, especially if one has been on its own for a long time.

Chinchillas should be of the opposite sex and have complimentary genes (see chapter on Chinchilla Genetics) otherwise the outcome could be problematic. Never put a new chinchilla straight into the cage of another, the present chinchilla will protect its territory and may attack the new intruder!

You should begin by putting the new chinchilla into its own cage next to the present chinchilla. Do not have the cages touching at this stage or they may bite one another through the wires, some are known to loose their toes this way (not a great introduction!).

Slowly over a 7 day period bring the cages closer together so eventually they are touching. Observe the behaviour of both chinchillas, if you see signs of aggression move the cages further apart and repeat the process until they are choosing to sit near one another in their respective cages.

By keeping the cages together for 2 weeks (touching one another), each chinchilla will have the chance to become accustomed to the smell and sight of the other. This may seem like a slow process but it is a sure way that the chinchillas will have a chance of pairing when they physically meet one another.

When both chinchillas are comfortable to be near one another it is now time to let them have physical contact. It is a good idea at this stage to check the female is not 'in season', as if she is all the male will try to do is mate with her. This will not please the female who will most probably turn around and attack in defence.

Females are generally the most dominant and can potentially kill their male counterparts, if a female rejects her male companion she will show her defensiveness by standing up on her hind legs and spraying urine at him before attacking if he does not get the initial message.

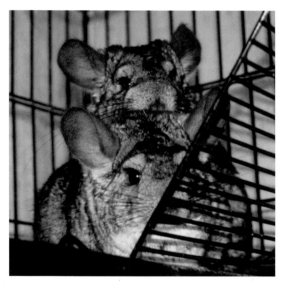

When chinchillas have been introduced properly, they generally live well together. Jasper & Rugrat.

The first meeting should be on neutral territory like a floor. If the present chinchilla has been allowed to run free, find a new space it has not seen for the introductions otherwise he/she will class this as its territory and may become aggressive. Stay in the room at all times and observe the behaviour.

Chinchillas usually start off by investigating their new surroundings and seem uninterested in meeting until they bump into one another. At this point, if there are any signs of aggression or a chase starts up, return the chinchillas to their respective cages immediately and try again the next night. Continue this way until they bump into one another and are happy to have a sniff and continue on their respective ways.

Allow this exercise period to continue over a couple of weeks, returning them to their own cages before trying to place them in the same one. It is best not to rush this period if you want calm in their new home, eventually you will find them sitting next to one another in their own cages, pining to be with one another (hopefully!).

When they seem comfortable and content to be near one another choose which cage they are to live in. If possible, it is best to place them in a completely new cage but if this is not feasible the cage you choose will need to be cleaned and present objects should be removed.

This method prevents territorial quarrels but some owners have been successful by placing the male immediately into the females existing cage. Remember females can kill and if you see her rear up and spray her intruder take him out immediately before he is attacked.

Place new toys in the cage and ensure there are places to hide, this will help them become more interested in their surroundings rather than one another at first and will get them used to one anothers presence. Place both animals in the new cage and watch them carefully. Some say this is best in the morning when they are tired and are more likely to go to sleep than fight but anytime is a good time to start.

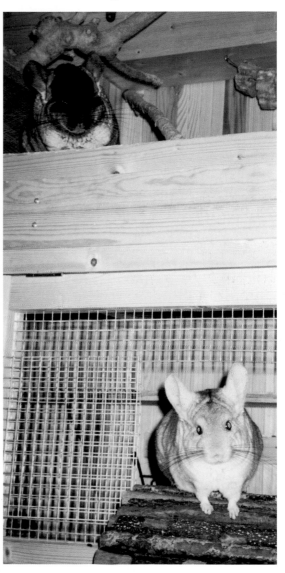

Do not worry if you hear a few noises or there is a small scuffle, this is just them trying to sort out living arrangements and what they like and do not like-just keep watching!

It is unwise to separate chinchillas unless you see them use their teeth or blood is drawn. If this happens you will need to separate both chinchillas into individual cages and begin the process again the next night, until they are finally sitting next to one another on the same shelf in the same cage.

Chinchillas need time to get used to one another and in a cage with no escape it is imperative that they get on. Placing some objects that can help them hide always helps. I try and remember how I would behave if an intruder came and broke into my house!

If they seem to be getting on well, it is a good idea to give them both a bath in their new

Cheeky & Sweetie in cage.

cage, this will help them relax and jump into one anothers sand. After a couple of hours and only when you see them sitting near to one another can you leave them.

On the first few nights it is wise to keep a regular check, just in case something happens but generally as soon as they are cuddled up together they have accepted one another and are more than happy to live together.

Two chinchillas chewing on a body scrub.

I can not stress enough the importance of not leaving chinchillas alone together until you have seen them accept one another by sitting closely side by side.

Some owners choose an alternative method that can work just aswell. They place a smaller wire cage inside a bigger cage and place a chinchilla in each.

The chinchillas are left this way for a couple of hours then the door of smaller cage is opened, if there is no hostility the smaller cage is then removed. They continue to be observed until they are sitting comfortably next to one another.

If they fight or act aggressively, the one who is showing the aggressive behaviour will be the one who is put inside the smaller of the two cages. This acts as a form of punishment until the next time they are introduced together. Care needs to be taken with this method otherwise you may find lost toes due to attacks.

Never let a first bad attempt from introducing chinchillas put you off. If you give them time and follow the correct methods you will get there in the end. Eventually your chinchillas will form a bond and their behaviours will eventually be influenced by what the other is doing.

MATING CHINCHILLAS

When breeding chinchillas it is imperative that you read every book, look at every website and ask for lots of advice to help be prepared and save yourself any heartache of missed signs of complications.

Chinchillas mate for life, when they have decided to live with one another fighting generally never occurs unless the female comes into 'season', even then the fighting will be moderate as long as your chinchillas have a place to hide and get away from one another.

They are very sensitive and highly susceptible to stress therefore if the environment feels insecure a female will not mate no matter how much the male tries!

Although they are sexually mature from 8 months, a chinchilla should never be breed until they are least at one year old. Even though they can conceive the internal organs are still not mature enough to handle a pregnancy and may result in birthing difficulties.

It has been suggested that waiting until a chinchilla is 2 - 3 years old is healthier for both the chinchilla and its offspring due to:

1) The reduced chance of suffering malocclusion and passing it on to kits (see Health Guide).
2) Temperament is evident and well established.
3) They have a reduced chance of passing on fur chewing if they are not one themselves, which would be apparent at this age.
4) Females are known to raise a healthier litter, as fertility in both males and females is more established.
5) The female will have a better ability to deal with the birth and future dependants.

Zena – Homo Ebony, Female and her kit Misty – TOV White Ebony, Female.

On the contrary some reports suggest that leaving a female 2-3 years without having any offspring will cause her to find it hard to deliver, due to immaturity. This may cause serious complications that may result in a caesarean section.

Therefore, if you are thinking of breeding, I will leave it to you to decide when it is the best time for you to breed your chinchillas based on the information above.

Remember one fact still remains - A chinchilla should never be breed before it is one year old!

To carry a kit to full term the females pelvic size should be measured by a vet to ensure the pelvic has developed fully and is big enough to carry a kit to full term. If the womb is too small, a female will have a difficult birth resulting in C-Section or maybe death.

A female generally comes into 'estrus' approximately every 30-40 days. Although a female may be in 'season' she may not always ovulate each time. This should be taken into account and therefore offspring may not be guaranteed after mating.

Females do not loose blood therefore they do not have a menstrational cycle. When

Blackie – Ebony, Male.

a female is in 'season' the opening of her vagina (normally closed) will become more apparent, this will stay open ready for copulation for 5 days from date of opening, accompanied by the excretion of a 'Heat Plug'.

The waxy 'Heat Plug' (approx 1-2cm) is excreted 1 day before the start of seasoning and consists of hardened vaginal fluids. It is rarely found by the owner and should not be confused with the 'Copulation Plug' (mentioned later in this chapter).

It is not too hard to tell when a female is 'in-season', as she will become more irritable and the male will become more attentive. He will display signs of alertness towards his female companion, nuzzling her and sniffing at her. A male may even become excited and start to wag his tail sideways accompanied by the squeaking and cooing sounds of the mating call (see chapter on Vocal Sounds of a Chinchilla).

When the 'Heat Plug' is finally released the fun usually commences with a mad chase around the cage with the male in hot pursuit.

Mating will generally occur at night or the early hours of the morning, as in the wild days, this time was safer and helped prevent predators killing their new-born kits.

Females will generally try to hide from her male companion until her receptive period has passed. Therefore if you want to force breed you should remove any hiding spaces from inside the cage. Remember though by doing this they will have nowhere to hide if things get aggressive or potentially deadly.

For a more natural conception the cage should not be tampered with, as this will make the female more secure and more likely to want to copulate (breed) on her own accord. You should leave hiding places as they are and observe their actions to ensure no aggression is present.

On the initial meeting a female will at first resist her mate's advances by biting his fur, barking and squirting urine at him.

After a short time the female will become more receptive and will then continue to mate on numerous occasions within a short amount of time. When mating has occurred, the male vocalises a sound similar to hiccups (see chapter on Vocal Sounds of a Chinchilla). If heard this is a sure guarantee that copulation has just taken place.

It is important after mating that you check the male to see that he can retract his penis back into the protection of the foreskin. A male chinchilla can develop hair around the penis during copulation known as 'Hair Ring'.

Hair Ring generally occurs in inexperienced or over sexed males. It can be extremely painful and if left unattended will cause death.

The accumulation of hair wrapped around the penis cannot be removed by the male, therefore causing the penis to dry out, turn black, shrivel and waste away.

The male will become lethargic, have trouble walking, lay on his side and refuse to move and eat. Hair Ring should never be left to this stage and the penis should always be checked as soon as you know copulation took place to prevent this potential agony (see Health Guide - Hair Ring).

After 24 hours of mating, the 'Copulation Plug' (Vaginal Plug/Covering Plug) is excreted from the female and measures approx. 2½ cm long (longer than the Heat Plug). It comprises of both hardened vaginal fluid and seminal fluid and is creamy-yellow in colour. The 'Copulation Plug' will stay inside the female vagina for 24 hours after mating. This is to prevent the male's sperm from being excreted before fertilisation has had a chance to take place.

The sign of the 'Copulation Plug' means that mating has occurred. It is not a guarantee that the female will have babies but is a good indication, approx 99% of the time your female will produce babies approximately 111days later.

The discovery of the 'Copulation Plug' is also the day known as conception date.

GESTATION PERIOD/PREGNACY

A chinchilla can get pregnant up to 3 times a year and may increase the size of the litter as they get older.

The gestation period is on average 111 days although this can range between 109-120 days.

Females generally produce two kits on average but provisions must be made as they can have anything up to six kits in one litter (very rare).

The early noticeable signs of a pregnant chinchilla include increases in water consumption, changes in food appetite and personality.

A female may become 'touchy' or 'snappy' towards her male mate and seem more tired. She will increase in weight & size, exhaust quicker after exercise and sleep in a more comfortable position, generally on her side.

It is debatable whether it is wise to weigh your chinchillas during pregnancy, as they should be undisturbed as much as possible to avoid miscarriage or injury to the foetuses. A helpful tip if you want to keep an eye on your pregnant female's weight gain is to place the scales inside the cage. Curiosity will generally cause her to jump on the scales giving you enough time to make a note of her weight.

Never pick up a pregnant female by the base of her tail, by doing so will spontaneously cause miscarriage, therefore if you must handle the female, pick her up gently cupping her into your hands supporting her rear.

Mopsi – A silver mosaic, pregnant female who's taking a 5 minute rest.

Females who generally liked to be cuddled by their human partners may not be impressed if you try to do so at this time.

Unless a chinchilla is having pregnancy difficulties, under no circumstance should the stomach be pushed, felt or investigated for babies.

A qualified vet or an extremely experienced breeder should only examine a pregnant chinchilla. By holding a chinchilla incorrectly or investigating her stomach you can not only affect the development of the foetus/es but also more drastically unnecessary miscarriage can occur.

A proper diet is essential to a female at times of pregnancy. Limit the amount of treats you give and increase fresh pellets and hay amounts also ensuring there is a fresh supply of water daily.

Supplements should be given cautiously during pregnancy and only on the recommendation of a qualified vet.

Some breeders have been known to give their pregnant female half a Tums tablet for extra calcium, which is an essential mineral to both the female and the unborn kits. Giving a female half of a Tums tablet daily may even help her kits against dental problems (seek a qualified vet for advise first).

Many females tend to loose weight during pregnancy due to lessened interest in food, do not be too alarmed if this happens it is quite natural, only keep an eye out for dramatic weight losses, protruding bones or severe weakness which can signal pregnancy abnormalities. If you are ever unsure always check with a vet.

It is extremely important that the female remains in her familiar surroundings and not placed somewhere new, as this will completely stress her and can be potentially disastrous. Some females have been known to simultaneously abort and then eat the dead babies after being moved to a new home.

Unless a male becomes increasingly aggressive towards a pregnant female, it is best if he remains in the cage with her during the gestation period. This will help him bond with the babies and help look after them when they are born. If he is shunted out at this stage he may become aggressive towards the female and her kits on his return.

Nearer the birth you will notice that the female's six nipples are more exposed and she will begin to busy herself building a nest to prepare for the event. The female will tend to use the lower level of a double story cage as a safe home for her kits and will collect hay, woodchips and bedding to make her nest for them.

Approximately 10 days before the expected birth date until approximately 10 days after, it is important that the female does not enjoy a dust bath. Harmful bacteria can be present in dust/sand and cause infection or inflammation of the vagina or womb causing devastating affects to the mother and newborn. Any dustbaths in the accommodation should be removed and stored until after the birth.

PREPARING FOR THE BIRTH

Firstly and most importantly you will need to ensure that the wire mesh around the cage has holes no larger than ¼" x ¼" (6mm x 6mm). Kits are extremely small and can squeeze easily through the smallest of spaces, therefore if the holes are larger than this, tape cardboard around the outside of the cage to ensure the kits do not fall through, escape or die.

If you have a solid bottom floor cage there is no need to worry but if your cage is made up of wire mesh with a drop through tray, then the holes cannot be bigger than ¼"x ¼" (6mm x 6mm)! Kits can even break their legs on these small openings so it is also wise to place untreated pine planks of wood, cardboard or a pieces of carpet around the cage until the kits have grown and are not in danger of getting a foot entangled within the openings.

Ensure cardboard is placed around the outside of the cage to prevent young kits from falling through.

Chinchillas are born with no conception of height, therefore cages with multi-floors should be concealed until the kits are bigger otherwise they will not be able to judge and will drop to lower levels, breaking limbs and potentially causing death.

Ensure all objects within the cage are sturdy so if any kits are inside and the chin-mum wants to jump about, she will not jump on something and kill her kits. Cardboard boxes at this stage should be removed and replaced with something more solid like a harmless wooden box or PVC pipes. Exercise wheels should also be removed until the kit is big enough to handle the operation.

Baby proof all areas of freedom which the kits may enter into, for example close all small gaps around skirting boards, between floorboards, under sofas etc. As they can squeeze through smaller gaps than their parents this must be taken into consideration if the kits are to run free and explore safety with no fatal consequences of being stuck within the cavities of a wall!

Ensure you are enlisted with a vet incase of birthing complications and that they are happy to come and visit at night if the unfortunate circumstance arose.

Ensure the room is at a constant temperature especially during the night, generally labour and birth start at this time and with central heating turned off rooms can become cold.

A kit will need to be kept warm (not hot!) therefore if there is no central heating then a heated nest box will be required.

A few days before birth you may notice the mother going completely off her food. She may drink more, produce soft droppings, stretch and become completely engrossed in perfecting her nest. This may then be followed by long periods of lazing about quietly waiting, do not worry these are all natural signs that the kits are on their way.

THE BIRTH

Chinchillas have been having successful births on their own in the wild for years so they should not really need any helping hands from us humans. It is important that you oversee the birth from a distance for complications but there is no need for interference unless difficulties arise.

Generally there are no major difficulties but if you feel the birth is becoming quite complicated or the mother is showing signs of stress or weakness, call the vet immediately - it is better to be safe than sorry!

There is no need to withdraw the male during labour or birth unless he is aggressive, he will aid the mother and attend to the kits with cleaning, drying and the afterbirth.

Most owners miss the miracles of the birth as the kits are mainly born in the night or early hours. A gestation chart will help you determine when the kits are due, so you can be there incase you are needed.

The beginning signs of labour show the female generally resting herself in the corner, the male at this stage should also not upset her as she will want to remain quiet.

Clio - in the first stages of labour.

When the contractions start up she will become increasingly uncomfortable and will be seen stretching together with audible murmurs.

Females generally rear up onto their hind legs cleaning the vaginal area that will now be open. The fur around the area will be evidently wet from the release of the birth fluid that may also be seen on the floor of the cage.

The labour stages are generally quite short and last approx 30 minutes to 1 hour.

When delivery begins you will see the female rise onto her hind legs and begin to contract. At this stage the pain is immense and she will be letting out loud squeals accompanied by teeth grinding.

When the kit's head is out, she will bend forward and start cleaning away the birth sac from the kits face, this is to ensure the face is clean and the sac is fully removed causing no blockages to breathing.

With her waters broken, this chinchilla is in the first stages of contractions.

Once the face has been cleaned the female will rise back onto her hind legs and push until the whole kit is out, sometimes aiding the birth with the gentle use of her teeth.

The whole birthing process can take anywhere between one or two hours with very little loss of blood. If at any point the labour is taking longer than two hours, contractions stop before the kit is out or substantial blood loss is evident, it is imperative that you contact a vet immediately who may assist the birth with a caesarean section.

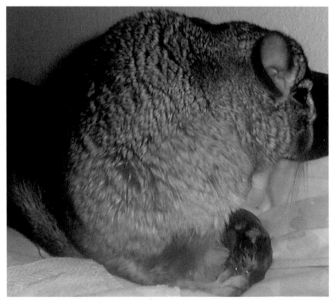

Clio in her final contraction – you can also see baby Loki emerging.

As soon as the kit is born, the female will attend to cleaning and drying it with the aid of her face and fur. This process is compulsory if the kit is to survive and not be left to dry on its own as it will die from cooling.

If the female is pre-occupied, the male will help at this stage in cleaning, drying, nudging and encouraging the kit to stand whilst she attends to herself.

The female will finally pull out any remains of

the birth sac with her teeth and then eat it before cleaning herself. At this stage she may deliver the afterbirth, depending on how many kits there are.

If there are to be more kits, the contractions for the second start shortly after the first birth, the same sequence will repeat itself of squealing, pushing, cleaning the kits face before finally pushing the second kit out completely. The birth sac will be removed and the process continued over and over again until all the kits are born and the final afterbirth is out.

A newborn kit just born, mother cleaning birthing sack under the watchful eye of Dad next door.

The afterbirth is generally eaten by the mother (father can eat it too) so it can not usually be found. It is small, fleshy and full of goodness to help replenish nutrients the mother has lost and includes hormones to help produce milk for feeding.

Delivery of only one afterbirth and having two kits will mean that the kits are twins, but if after a second kit there is another afterbirth, you can safety say they have developed individually and are independent kits.

When the mother is finally clean she will return to her kits, nudging them under her to encourage them to suckle and feed, aiding them to keep warm.

*This new mother has urged her kit underneath her to keep the kit warm and help in drying it out. *Note the afterbirth in the fore picture.*

After 4 hours you may want to very gently feel the chin-mums stomach, firstly to see if it is warm as if not she may not be producing enough milk to feed her kits. If this is the case you will need to rear the kits by hand (see chapter on Birthing Complications).

Secondly, if you feel any lumps and contractions have stopped you should contact a vet immediately, as there is an unfortunate chance a kit is still inside.

It is important to keep an eye on the male immediately after the final afterbirth is delivered as the female will come straight into 'season' and will be able to conceive again. For the first 5-7 days after birth, the father should be removed from the cage or only left with the female under your supervision if 'back-breeding' is to be prevented.

Clio eating the nourishing after birth.

Back breeding is potentially very dangerous to both the female chinchilla and the unborn kits. It occurs when a female immediately becomes pregnant with a second litter straight after giving birth to the first. A lactating female will be exhausted from feeding her new-born kits and will not be able to provide the proper nutrients required for the unborn kits growing inside her.

The subsequent birth can carry many complications and may result in a caesarean section. The mother will be drained of energy from her present litter and may not have enough exertion for the next delivery; consequently back-breeding should always be prevented.

If you are ever seriously worried about any issues arising from the birth you should always call a vet immediately.

This wet newborn kit is ready to explore immediately and goes to meet his Dad.

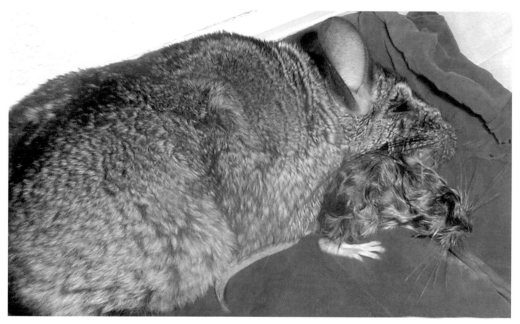

Clio and Loki resting shortly after the birthing process.

BIRTHING COMPLICATIONS

Pregnant chinchillas rarely have difficult births but if any difficulties should arise or the female is looking exhausted you should call your vet immediately if either the chinchilla or the kits are to survive.

The female will yelp with contractions which is normal but if you spot your chinchilla having a contraction followed by stretching up on hind legs then squatting this is a sure sign of a breech birth and a vet should be called immediately.

Excessive vocal sounds during labour may indicate another sign of a birthing complication

A heat lamp directed into the cage is a good way of keeping a newborn kit warm.

Occasionally the onset of another set of contractions may happen before the female has cleaned and dried her newborn. If the father is present he will generally take over this role, however, in some situations a father will choose to neglect the kit that will then need immediate help if it is to survive and this is the only stage that you will really need to intervene.

Juliet – missing her nipple after sibling rivalry had one kit hanging on as the other pulled him off taking the nipple with him. The fur has been pulled out trying to find the nipple and fighting amongst the kits.

You should gently remove the kit, cupping it in your hands and gently breathe regularly into its face to aid respiration. Keeping the kit gently held in your hands will aid in warming the kit. When it is able to stand on its own gently dry him with a clean towel (watch you do not break any tiny bones with roughness) and place it back into the cage immediately so it can be with its mother.

Unfortunately there are occasional sad incidences where a kit will be 'still born', perhaps due to being part of a large litter and not receiving relevant nutrients for growth or being the last one out which took too long. Sadly, it is quite common for the mother to disregard the newborn and sometimes (although rare) may even attack it.

Litters generally comprise of 2-3 kits but very occasionally the litter can be larger, in these instances a mother can become quickly exhausted with the traumas of labour and will need a medical helping hand to remove the remaining kits.

Most situations involving a complicated birth will end up with the female having a Caesarean Section (see Health Guide) and it is a sad fact that unless immediate attention is sort, most kits will die either in their mothers womb or shortly after birth.

It is always essential that if the situation is becoming complicated or you are unsure if the female is in distress, you call a qualified vet immediately, therefore, you should be registered with a practitioner and have his number at hand when you know the female is pregnant.

RAISING KITS

Healthy kits are born with their eyes open, their bodies covered in fur and teeth present.

A healthy kit will weigh between 35-60 grams (2-2½ oz) at birth and will grow rapidly. Kits born at weights of 30 grams or less are classed as small and unfortunately kits under 25 grams are very weak and generally have a lessened chance of survival.

Usually within an hour of birth the kit is dry, feeding from the chin-mum and is wandering about exploring! (Remember that it is important that the floor is secure and covered to ensure kits do not get any limbs entangled between the bars).

During the first 7 days you may not see the kits much if they were born in a hiding space, however, they will venture out for the quick exploration but will generally stay tucked up under the chin-mum staying warm and feeding. It is imperative that there is an ample supply of fresh daily food for the mother to help her produce plenty of milk for the kits and that they are left undisturbed as much as possible.

It is also essential that you observe the weight of the kits during the first few weeks, as one who is not feeding adequately will die from malnutrition and starvation in a couple of days of birth if not helped.

Kits can be quite mean and aggressive towards their siblings especially if there are three of them or more, this is usually down to the food supply. If you find this is happening check the female's stomach to see how many nipples are being used.

Balding may be evident around the nipples the kits have chosen to feed from. If you see balding around only a couple of the nipples it may mean a kit cannot find the others amongst the chin-mums dense fur or is being pushed out by it's siblings. In either case action must be immediately taken.

The excess fur around the nipples will need to be carefully trimmed for a weakened kit to be able to feed, this should only ever be done by a qualified vet as it can be easy to cut into the chin-mums nipple.

1 week old - Lauren - Dark Tan, Female.

If this does not rectify the problem on the very next feed then you will need to separate the kits during feeding times by removing the more aggressive ones and allowing the weaker kits to feed first. This must be done twice a day for at least 4 weeks or until you notice good weight gain via weighing scales (5-10 grams a week). If a kit is becoming increasingly weak call a vet immediately.

Kits must be feeding from their chin-mum within 24 hours from birth if it has chance of survival or it will just cuddle her, choosing to not eat and starve to death even if it is on its own with her with no sibling rivalry.

An alternative is to feed the kit yourself via a pipette although care must be taken to ensure there is no chokage or suffocation from milk that may enter the nasal passage. Ask your vet for a milk combination which you can use and if you are unsure ask the vet to show you how to administer feeding to your new kit. It has been said that evaporated milk mixed with camomile tea is similar to chinchilla milk (2 parts tea: 1 part milk). Remember: It is imperative that you have a kit feeding within 24 hours of birth.

If you are ever going to lose a kit, it will generally be within the first week of birth, they say you can tell a kit's health in its first few days by the tail.

When kits are first born their tail is completely straight and looks like it is dragging along the floor, within 12 hours it should be kinking up at the end and by 48 hours the tail should curl up in the air. This is a sure way of ensuring your kit is feeding and is healthy.

It is a good idea to handle kits if they are to get used to human contact. You must be careful when handling a kit for two reasons. Firstly, kits have small bones which can easily break if held too hard and secondly, they are quick and have no concept of height so watch they do not fall or hop out of your hands and drop to the floor causing death.

Handling a kit will give you more opportunities than just them getting used to your hands. It also gives you an opportunity to feel their tummies to ensure it is warm and full, therefore receiving milk, together with a chance to weigh the kits and keep a weekly record to ensure they are gaining a regular weight of between 5-10 grams (per week) and growing normally.

A kit at this age should only digest milk, never give a kit treats or pellets as their digestive tract is ultra sensitive and the food will not be digested easily causing the kit to become ill and potentially die.

Standard male, 3 months old.

You can also check for any sibling rivalry from bites or cuts to their body, if this is so, bathe the area in warm water, dry gently and apply an extremely small amount of antiseptic cream to the area. Gently rub the cream in so the kit cannot digest it afterwards.

Stormy – Homo Ebony, Male, Flurry – White Ebony Male & Winter – Homo Ebony Female, all kits are 3 days old.

After 7 days the kits will become more active and inquisitive, you will hear their unique cries to the chin-mum to let them know where they are and the mother will respond (see chapter on Vocal Sounds of a Chinchilla).

You must ensure that any shelves or ledges which kits have access to be of a safe drop (approx 35cms or less), otherwise it can lead to broken bones or worst, death! Kits are renowned for climbing the sides of the cage and letting go when they hit the top...ouch!

It is wise not to give a kit a dustbath for its first 7-10 days, as they do not know what to do with it and will generally end up in a right mess with an eye infection. After the chin-mums first bath on her own, you can also allow the kits to take their first bath. Place a dustbath in the cage for the chin-mum, making sure it is big enough to accommodate the kits and let the chin-mum show her kits what to do. The kits will become extremely curious and will join in the game enthusiastically.

At 4 weeks kits begin to nibble on small amounts of hay and pellets, it is wise to give the chin-mum her food at a height that cannot be reached by the kits as their main source of nutrition at this stage should still be their mothers milk. A kit that over eats on pellets at this age will die.

At 8 weeks kits can begin to increase their intake of pellets to ½ - ¾ tablespoons daily and commence weaning from their mother. They can

Panda- White Mosaic, Female.

also come out of their cage environment and explore the extra surroundings you have created. Remember they are still extremely small under all that fur and can squeeze into the smallest of spaces! They will still break bones if they fall from a height and will inevitably die at this age if they consume something unhealthy, therefore double check the area is completely safe before letting them run free.

It is helpful to the mother having the father about as he is happy to help out cleaning and attending to the kits as well as giving the chin-mum some truly deserved time to herself. It is very occasional that a chin-dad will act aggressive to any of the litter but if this is the case, he should remain in his own cage, next to the chin-mum and returned after the kits have been weaned.

POST NATAL CARE

Extra care should be given to the new chin-mum as she nurses her kits and gains back the strength she has lost due to labour.

Ensure her environment is stress free and extra quiet so she can sleep whenever possible. It is said that giving a new mum some diluted cranberry juice will help recovery by adding valuable antioxidants into the diet, aiding milk flow and replenishing some of the lost vitamins due to the birthing process.

Do not worry if you see some fur around the nipples thinning or missing it is just where the kits have been suckling and have worn away the fur, this will grow back in no time.

Refrain from giving a dustbath to the chin-mum for the first 10 days to allow for the healing of the womb so no

Eileen with her Kits having their first bath at 10 days old.

infections occur and avoid handling her as much as possible during the nursing weeks.

It is suggested that you should give a lactating chin-mum extra calcium but this should be checked with your vet before initiating. Also, if at any point the chin-mum begins to look exhausted, extra thin or unwilling to feed her kits, a vet should be called immediately for treatment.

WEANING

Weaning from the chin-mums milk is usually decided by the chin-mum herself, but if a kit has not started by 8 weeks you will need to help the weaning process along.

There are several factors to consider about the best age to wean kits from their mother and living quarters all depending on who is living in the cage at the time.

If the chin-dad is in the same cage then both male and female kits need to be removed at 8 weeks (no sooner or later) to prevent in-breeding between parents and the offspring. Chinchillas have no concept of being related to one another therefore, it is important that you prevent any chances of this type of breeding to occur.

If the chin-dad is in another cage then the male kits should be separated from their mother at 8 weeks (no sooner or later) as it will be possible to impregnate their chin-mum. Female kits can

Duffy - Standard male and his 4 weeks old Standard baby boy.

remain until the chin-dad returns or if the chin-mum becomes dangerously aggressive towards her female offspring. I know of a family of chinchillas consisting of mother, daughter and aunty and they all still live happily together but this is not always the case so care should always be taken.

It is best to place the kits of the same sex into a communal cage rather than on their own. This helps develop their social behaviour and eases any stress of leaving their chin-mum. By separating the male and female kits it also lessens the chance of any in-breeding which can be fatal, just as fatal as getting pregnant at 4-5 months which is also possible and equally devastating!

Kits should then be monitored during the first days of weaning and if

Harmony – TOV Beige/Violet surrogate mum to Paisley – Male 2 months.

the chin-mum still has any milk, you should return the kits to their mother once or twice a day for a feed and reduce visits as days go on. By two weeks a kit should be fully weaned from its mothers milk.

A pair of kits small enough to fit into the palm of their owners hand.

You must ensure you provide ¾ - 1 tablespoon of pellets a day and no more until they are 6 months old. After 6 months you can slowly increase the portions to an adult size of 2 tablespoons per day. Never ever give treats to a kit under 4 months and only ¼ tsp. thereafter. A kit should never be sold immediately after it is weaned from its mother and it should never be weaned early for a quick sale.

It is seriously detrimental to take a kit from its original environment earlier than 12 weeks if good health is to be promoted. A kit taken too early from its mother can inherit fur biting and under developed social skills.

SELLING KITS

I shall only briefly touch on this subject as I feel too much information will be geared towards breeders who need to know more information than this book contains. Information for breeding chinchillas for the purpose of selling involves a lot more responsibility and further research should be undertaken.

I also hope that by not delving too deeply, a new chinchilla owner will steer away from this hobby and prevent an epidemic of chinchillas ending up in rescue homes.

Selling kits is best left to the breeders we have today but should you find you have extra chinchillas on

Loki – Standard Grey, 6 hours after birth.

your hands, it is imperative that you find out about the future owners' intentions.

You can place adverts in your local pet shop or newspaper and ask potential owners to visit in the evenings when the chinchillas are at play. This will give you the opportunity to see how the future owner handles the chinchilla.

It is wise to ask why they would like a chinchilla, who the chinchilla is for and how much knowledge they have. Never sell a chinchilla to a young child or to someone who is not prepared to give it potentially 10 years of company.

Ask the future owner about the housing

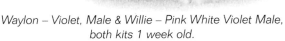

Waylon – Violet, Male & Willie – Pink White Violet Male, both kits 1 week old.

arrangements for the chinchilla (i.e. where it is to be kept, how big is the cage etc.) and whether the chinchilla is being purchased for a pet or breeding purposes. It is best to only sell a chinchilla for breeding purposes to someone who is experienced.

If you do not wish to have the responsibility of selling kits then the best bet is to get the male castrated.

CASTRATING A MALE CHINCHILLA

There are some reasons for castrating a male, the most obvious being the prevention of unwanted kits. This could be due to the owner not wanting the complications of breeding or the chin-pair could hold fatality genes which could be potentially harmful if they were to mate (see chapter on Chinchilla Genetics).

It is also sometimes needed to stop unwanted kits that could then become potentially neglected and die or an epidemic spreading to the rescue homes but either way the decision should not be taken lightly and all possible consequences should be considered carefully.

The details provided in this chapter includes the pros and cons of chinchilla castration with some anecdotal evidence and is also intended to help you make an informed choice about this matter.

There are many factors involved when thinking about castration, as most importantly chinchillas do not come round from the anaesthetic very well if at all!

As chinchillas are small rodents, giving them anaesthetic must be done with caution as it will not need much to kill them from overdose or shock (see Health Guide). If you are considering castration you must first ensure the vet you choose has expert knowledge of small rodents especially chinchillas under anaesthetic - if not do not chance it and find another veterinary practice that does!

A vet will need to perform the operation quickly and efficiently to give the male any chance of survival. He must be aware of the chinchilla's anatomy as the groin area of a chinchilla is open therefore it will need closing as well as the testicles removed. If the groin is left open the bowels of the male will drop into the scrotum sack cutting off blood supply and causing immense pain and death.

After a chinchilla has been castrated he can wear a collar to

Waylon – Violet, Male & Willie – Pink White Violet Male, both kits 1 week old.

prevent him infecting the wound by chewing it, the collar should be left on for 10-14 days and only be removed when the wound is healed and clean. You can ask a vet to place the collar on before you collect him to reduce any further stress to the male when he gets home.

If the operation is successful (and many are) you will generally be able to pick your chinchilla up after 4 hours. During this time, prepare his cage for arrival by ensuring it has been sterilised to eliminate any harmful bacteria that can cause infection and supply fresh food and water placed low in the cage.

You should place only essential items in the cage at this time to ensure the male can roam freely without banging the operated area. Ensure he has got a solid place to rest that will be more comfortable than a wired floor and the cage is in a dark, peaceful room.

Picking the male up from his operation is always heart rendering as you will be so relieved that he has come through the dangers of the anaesthetic only to be greeted by a sorrowful, limp state with his tiny back legs crossed. He will not be grateful....No, (unless it was life saving) but you are already half way there to recovery.

On arrival home, you will need to pick your chinchilla up gently and place him back into his sterilised warm home. I would most definitely advise a treat here, but not too much as his stomach is still tender from the anaesthetic and may not digest the treat well but one raisin will help and deter any pain from potential constipation. Do not be upset if your male does not take the treat at this stage as he has just been through a major ordeal in its little life, but keep an eye on him and offer a treat at hourly intervals of recovery until he accepts it.

Excellent care and attention needs to be performed if any male is to recover fully. You should keep the male quiet, calm and warm and regularly check on him when he first arrives home. The male will seem limp at first and will lay on his side with his back legs crossed not moving much, so during this time he should be checked every 20 minutes to ensure he has not fallen into a coma from the anaesthetic.

The male will be looking sorry for himself for approximately 4 days after the operation and when he first gets up he will be wobbly and unbalanced. He will not be able to jump on top of houses or onto shelves very well so food must be easily accessible. Over these next 12-18 hours, the male should be checked every 40 minutes to ensure he is coming through the effects of anaesthetic satisfactorily. After 24 hours, consumption of eating and drinking should be returning to normal.

I would advise against a dust bath until the wound is fully healed and cleared, usually after 10-14 days.

If the male is accommodated in a pair, it is up to you if you want to put the male straight back in with the female after the operation. If you do, observe the females reaction and if she starts to reject the male or nibbles at the wound, remove her into another cage.

There is mixed feedback of placing chinchillas together straight after an operation. One side states that the female will comfort the recovering male, whilst the other says the female will reject the male as he will be carrying vet odours and will smell like an intruder. If you are unsure it is best to place the male in with the female and observe his reactions.

Should the chinchillas need separating,

Leo – Dark tan, Male, 4 months old.

it is best to leave the male in the familiar cage to ease further stress or shock of being in an unknown environment. After 2 weeks and the male chinchilla has bathed well (all odour from the veterinary surgery MUST be removed from the male if successful re-introduction is to happen) you can reintroduce the pair and observe how they get on (see chapter on Introducing Chinchillas).

I have heard some stories of chinchilla owners who have had their pets castrated successfully whilst others have had

Mucki – Beige, Male.

further problems, here are a few stories to help make up your mind.

A woman owned two chinchillas (one female and one male) she decided to get the male castrated to prevent unwanted kits. She felt absolutely awful in putting the male through the operation and was beside herself with worry. He successfully made the operation but unfortunately the female then rejected him due to not being able to perform his functional duties! (although this is uncommon)

Another woman went through the same agonising guilt in putting her male through castration to prevent unwanted kits, only to find that the stress of the ordeal then gave him behaviour problems and bouts of severe depression.

Again the same indecision applied to the third lady who was concerned about the best thing to do. When she finally came to the decision to have the male castrated she took him to the vet only to never pick him up again....he died during the surgery unable to cope with the anaesthetic!

The stories above can be very familiar but saying this there are many successful castrations where the male will continue to live a happy, healthy existence with his female companion.

To help the survival of the male you must ensure he is never castrated under 8 months and he is of good weight on a healthy diet of pellets and hay.

It is best to always postpone the operation if you think the male is unwell or not on his best form. It is never worth the risk if you are unsure; being told your chinchilla is dead when you only tried to do the best is not something you will wish to live with!

GERIATRIC CARE

Chinchillas will generally keep their loveable bouncy character well into old age although some do become slightly slower. Some owners mention that their chinchillas become more loveable and enjoy cuddles more often as they get older but this I would suggest is down to individual characteristics and not all will be the same.

You should ensure you are gentle when picking up geriatrics as their bones will be weaker and more easily broken and never put them in a potential stress situation.

As they get older it is sometimes recommended to introduce calcium tablets within their diet to help against weak bones. Vitamin C can also be added to provide antioxidants into the body to help fight illnesses or disease (if you have not already done so), but always check supplements first with your vet.

Should a chinchilla reach a ripe old age and getting about the cage is becoming more difficult, it may be time to change the layout or design of the cage to prevent falls and broken bones.

Access to higher levels should be made easier and remove objects that could potentially be harmful, as generally whenever a chinchilla hurts him/herself in such a manner the only way to conduct a complete examination is to anaesthetise the chinchilla.

Remember chinchillas do not take well to anaesthetic at the best of times and any such ordeal at an old age will almost certainly cause death to the animal, therefore eliminate any potential risks to ensure the health and safety of the elders.

It is recommended that you examine your pet on a more regular basis and monitor the weight weekly.

You may notice your vet bills increase slightly as your chinchilla gets older and needs more care, it is also useful to know if your vet will conduct home visits (although more costly) as you may want to reduce the stress by having him visited in its own environment. (One of my chinchillas takes two days to get over a visit to the vets and he's only 2!).

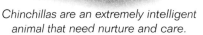

Chinchillas are an extremely intelligent animal that need nurture and care.

Providing you are confident that your older chinchilla is receiving the correct balance of nutrition, regular check-ups and weigh-ins together with a safer environment there is no reason why he/she should not lead a happy healthy later life.

HEALTH ISSUES

Chinchillas are generally robust little animals but they are susceptible to certain illnesses (see Health Guide) and should be routinely checked by yourself weekly if early stages are to be diagnosed.

If ever you suspect an illness or health issue you should always contact your vet (who should be qualified in dealing with chinchillas or small rodents).

Never leave any symptoms unchecked, usually when signs become more noticeable the chinchilla is in the latter stages of the illness/disease and is less likely to be treated and more prone to death.

CARING FOR A SICK CHINCHILLA

Very occasionally your chinchilla will need extra care, it is not very often they become sick (providing you have supplied a healthy diet and regime) but when they do it is vital you take the correct care to ensure speedy recovery.

Always give a sick chinchilla plenty of peace and quiet within a dark warm environment and check on them regularly.

It is important that you provide a fresh supply of water, hay and pellets daily and their weight is monitored regularly.

Dustbaths should be suspended until the illness is over, unless stated otherwise by your vet.

The cage should be dry and clean at all times especially in sickness when a chinchilla's resistance is low and further infection is easily picked up.

Depending on what the cause of the illness is, you may ask your vet if you can offer any further supplements to your chinchilla to aid recovery. Monitor any medications prescribed for side effects (see Health Guide).

Always call a qualified vet if you are unsure of the cause or treatment. Avoid handling the chinchilla unnecessarily and follow all instructions provided by the vet vigorously.

FIRST AID KIT FOR A CHINCHILLA

It is wise to keep a first aid kit for your chinchilla that is easily accessible at all times. The kit should contain the following items:

A COLLAR made up of two hard pieces of cardboard, which are cut into semi circles that are then taped together around the chinchilla's head. You will need to ensure the inner hole is big enough to not choke the chinchilla and the outer radius is 3.6cm - 5cm (1½ - 2") wider than the inner radius.

A PEPETTE OR DROPETTE to feed water through if your chinchilla needs to be fed.

A MEASURING SYRINGE is used to extract liquid medicine from the bottle showing the amount before adding to the water.

GAUZE & BANDAGE for sensitive skin can be used in conjunction with a collar to stop the chinchilla chewing the item. It is wise to keep a small bandage in case a chinchilla cuts himself or rips a foot from getting it caught etc. to help ease blood flow until the vet is present for examination.

STICKY TAPE for bandage and gauze.

GENTLE ANTISEPTIC which can be used on children for cuts, sores or open wounds, can also be used on chinchillas providing they have the use of a collar to stop them digesting the ointment.

SCISSORS for cutting.

A TRAVELLING CAGE/BOX to take the chinchilla to the vetenary surgery.

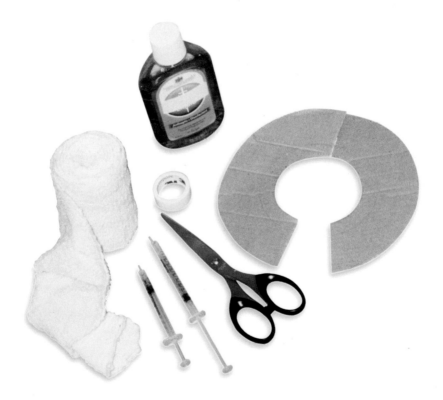

Items for a First Aid Kit.

QUESTIONS & ANSWERS

How much should a chinchilla cost?
Chinchillas can vary in price depending on their colour. At the time of printing this book, prices start from £45 for a standard grey or beige increasing to £100+ for a black ebony or pink white. (These prices are general guidelines and different colour mutations should fall within these price parameters).

Is a chinchilla a good pet for a child under 7 years old?
Depends! Although they are gentle animals that rarely bite, they like to be left alone in the daytime to sleep. Interrupted sleep will cause the animal to become stressed and illnesses to occur. Young children tend to grasp at things and grasping at a chinchilla will either cause it to loose its fur or break its tail/bones or worse death. As a child grows up they can be taught the responsibilities of looking after a chinchilla and can provide gentle interactive play with the animal, under adult supervision.

Can a chinchilla be introduced to my other pets?
Never should a chinchilla be introduced to anything other than its own kind! (see Health Guide - Stress). Some owners are successful at keeping both a chinchilla and a dog or cat but it is imperative that you never leave these animals alone together if fatalities to the chinchillas are to be prevented. Chinchillas also have nocturnal habits therefore any animal who does not adhere to this lifestyle will be detrimental to its heath. Never cage another animal in with a chinchilla even if it is another rodent!

How do I obtain a breeders telephone number?
Pet shops will use various breeders and therefore this is a good place to start. Ask the shop if you can have the telephone number of their local chinchilla breeder so you can arrange a meeting to view the herd and ask questions before purchase. If pet shops are reluctant to offer this information, your local veterinary surgery should be able to point you in further directions.

Are chinchillas expensive to keep as pets?
After initial expenditure of the cage and accessories a chinchilla is an inexpensive animal to keep. The only supplies needed are good quality pellets and hay and a pumice stone for their teeth. Cages vary in price but please do not let the price determine which cage you choose. A chinchilla should be housed in a minimum area of 18" (46cm) deep x 24"- 36" (61cm - 92cm) wide x 24"- 36" (61cm - 92cm) high.

How intelligent are chinchillas?
Chinchilla are extremely intelligent animals and have been compared to the intellectual level of the squirrel. They remember their way around things and

know if something has been moved. Remember that if you ever scare a chinchilla he will remember it for a quite a few days!

Where can I get some more information on chinchillas?
You can ask advice from both pet shops and breeders. Breeders can be an excellent source of information as too are vets. If you are on the Internet there are a lot of fantastic sites which will be able to help you obtain the relevant information you are looking for, ensure the site is reputable and consistent before following any action. (A list of excellent sites can be found in the reference section at the back of this book).

LAST WORD

It is my responsibility in writing this book that chinchillas are not perceived as just fluffy cute pets. They are becoming extremely popular and every care should be taken that these adorable creatures are not caught up in the "pets for presents" trade and then become unwanted!

Chinchillas look like cuddly round balls of fluff but this picture should not be the only reason to purchase one!

Chinchillas need great commitment, but there is a great personality inside. This personality will need constant attention, love and 2 hours (minimum) of your time every night if they are to thrive.

They are highly sensitive and can feel pain and rejection therefore every aspect of a chinchilla should be taken into consideration before purchasing one.

A rescue service will not look upon you favourably if you decide to buy a chinchilla then give it up, needless to say how distraught the chinchilla will be.

When thinking of buying a chinchilla think of its potential 10-15 year life span and remember:

A PET IS NOT A PRESENT, IT IS FOR LIFE. IT IS SOMETHING TO NURTURE AND CARE FOR.

If you have purchased this book on the basis of deciding whether a chinchilla is the best type of pet for you, then I hope the information has helped you come to the correct decision.

If you have decided after reading this book that purchasing a chinchilla is not the best thing you could do, then I am pleased that you have come to this decision, as this will be one less unwanted chinchilla!

However if you want to acquire a chinchilla then I can assure you with the right amount of care and attention from yourself and information from this book, your chinchilla should have a happy and comfortable life.

A-Z HEALTH GUIDE

The information that follows is only a general guide and does not replace vetenary advice which should always be sought on the first signs of illness.

Abscesses - Are generally caused from an infected cut or wound. The cause can be from fighting or a sharp unclean object in the cage.

Signs - An opening or wound which is inflamed, showing redness and yellow mucus. A closed abscess will be swollen, red and infected yellow.

Prevention - Chinchillas that are aggressive should be removed, isolated and re-trained. When cleaning the cage, sharp objects should be checked for regularly and the cage should be disinfected once a week.

Cures - A collar will need to be placed around the chinchilla's head preventing him from getting at the infected area. A vet will need to administer an initial antibiotic that will then need to be continued at home. Usually the treatment is for 5 days and no dustbaths should be given during this time and not until the wound has healed. If the infected area has become seriously bad, a vet may consider amputation, if so anaesthetic will need to be administered followed by a course of antibiotics.

Fatality Chance - MEDIUM-HIGH. If an abscess is left untreated and the chinchilla is able to get at it, he will then digest the mucus into the digestive system that can then cause digestive problems; the abscess may also spread and become untreatable. If an abscess is treated at first onset it will disappear and the chinchilla's health should return to normal.

Bad breath - See Diabetes

Bloating - This disorder is not well understood but it may indicate a severe infection from internal parasites (see Parasites), or contaminated food and water. In any case the symptoms should not be ignored and the chinchilla must be taken to a vet to provide fresh samples of droppings immediately.

Signs - A chinchilla will puff up like a balloon, droppings will be airy (holey), sticky and covered in mucus. There will be loss of energy and discomfort.

Prevention - A healthy diet with lots of exercise. Good cage sanitation and food hygiene. Prevention's that are used for parasites and worms should also be adhered to.

Cures - The chinchilla will need to be taken to a vet immediately for diagnosis, thereafter, you should provide more free exercise time outside the cage, good sanitation and food hygiene. Wherever possible boil drinking water and allow to cool for 20 minutes before providing it to a chinchilla.

Fatality Chance - UNKNOWN. There is not a lot of information regarding the causes of bloating therefore no risk should be taken. On first signs, it is wise to contact a vet immediately so diagnosis and treatment can begin.

Broken Bones or Tail - Chinchilla bones are tiny and therefore broken easily. Breakages can be from falling incorrectly from a specific height, holding or catching the rear legs or being hit by a falling object if escaped. Chinchillas are also prone to break their legs on wire mesh floors with holes larger than ¼" (6mm) square, causing the leg to become entangled as they jump and a fight to wriggle free. It has been known for a chinchilla to either completely sever its leg from its body or chew the leg off in an attempt to become free! Their tails are also weak and can be broken in doors or when held by the tip.

Chilli with her broken leg in a blue cast.

Signs - Walking with difficulty, nibbling or chewing at the area, protruding bones or a short tail.

Prevention - Ensure you know how to handle your chinchilla properly (*see chapter on Holding a Chinchilla*) and never pick or hold a chinchilla by the back legs or tip of the tail. If a wire bottom cage has spaces larger than ¼" x ¼" (6mm x 6mm) then place some untreated pine boards around the cage for the chinchilla to jump onto rather than directly onto the floor.

Cures - If the chinchilla's leg is entangled in the mesh floor, gently help to release it by holding the chinchilla firmly so it does not wriggle and slowly withdraw the leg from the hole. Place a collar around the pet, ensuring it is not too tight around the neck and contact a vet immediately who can administer plaster to the broken area or anti inflammatory tablets if the tail has snapped. A collar should be worn both before and after plaster is applied to ensure the chinchilla does not try and chew his bones or the covering plaster. This also applies to the tail area where the collar should not be removed until it has healed or the chinchilla may chew the area and infection will set in.

Fatality Chance - MEDIUM-HIGH. Although broken bones do not kill (other than the neck) it will seriously immobilise your pet, causing the chinchilla to become inactive, go off of food, become stressed and deteriorate in health.

Broken Teeth - (See also Malocclusion & Teeth) Generally it is only the incisors that can get broken. They get stuck and break between the wire mesh on cages as they are trying to retrieve something or if they fall against something hard.

Signs - Uneven teeth and pawing at the mouth. Wetness to fur around the mouth area due to dribbling. Ungroomed clumps of hair around the back of thighs.

Prevention - Clean wire bottom cages regularly, if a chinchilla smells dropped food in the tray below he will try to get at it causing the teeth to become caught within the wires.

Cures - A chinchilla will need to attend a vet for the teeth to be filed and smoothed. Do not attempt to do this yourself as it can cause immense pain to your chinchilla, generally a chinchilla will need to be anaesthetised by a vet before filing. If the chinchilla has fallen, have the vet check his jaw line.

Fatality Chance - MEDIUM-HIGH. Generally broken teeth will not kill, it is only if they are not filed and left sharp that it will become painful to the chinchilla causing him to withdraw from eating and potentially starve.

Broken Whiskers - (*see Fungus Infections*)

Caesarean Section- Will only happen in the event of a complicated pregnancy and is performed by making an incision through the abdominal wall and uterus enabling access to the unborn kit. This operation will be done under anaesthetic and the rules of caring for a sick chinchilla (see chapter on Caring for a Sick Chinchilla) will need to be adhered to if the female is to survive the ordeal.

Signs - Long labour with no production of kits, constant squawking or squeaking from a pregnant female in pain, large litters and stretching up on back legs will all be signs of a complicated birth. Whenever in doubt always call a vet, it is better to be safe than sorry!

Prevention - C-Section is difficult to prevent but ensuring the pregnant chinchilla receives correct nutrients and care from the onset of pregnancy will only help aid a healthy birth.

Cures - There are no cures but you can help the recovery time of a female after a C-Section by providing the correct care (*see chapter on Caring for a Sick Chinchilla*).

Fatality Chance -HIGH. If left too late the chances of both the kits and mother dying are extremely high.

Cancer - Can occur to the ears of light coloured chinchillas.

Signs - Black moles or patches of black mainly occurring on the ears.

Prevention - Avoid keeping the cage in direct sunlight and out of smoke filled rooms.

Cure - If caught in the very early stages a chinchilla will have a chance of survival. The treatment for latter stages is extremely harsh on a chinchilla's digestive tract; therefore chances of survival will be lessened.

Fatality Chance - HIGH. Treatment of cancer is generally intolerable to the chinchilla digestive tract therefore the chance of survival can be slim.

Coccidia - One of the harder internal parasites to kill (*see Parasites*). It lives in the intestines leaving eggs before invading the walls and entering the lymph system where it then divides. It can be caused from a dirty or unkept environment or contaminated food. Coccidia generally infects the liver or intestines.

Signs - Increased appetite, lethargy, diarrhoea (droppings extremely soft and mashed into shelves etc.), bloating.

Prevention - Wash hands before handling chinchilla food and supply fresh pellets twice a day. Provide water that has been boiled and cooled for 20 minutes. Keep the cage in good sanitation and sterilise regularly. Probiotics added to water will keep the gut functioning normally.

Cures - A vet will need a fresh stool sample to examine and will prescribe medication in order to kill the parasites, usually a course over 5-7 days. Fresh boiled water will need to be supplied to help hydration after diahorrea. Complete sterilisation to the cage is paramount, using strong disinfectant and washed well with water. Anything that cannot be disinfected (i.e. wooden houses, carpets, wooden toys or hideaways) must be thrown away or replaced. Provide a fresh supply of pellets and hay (preferably alfalfa which has 18+ % protein to help build up the chinchilla).

Fatality Chance - HIGH. If untreated eventually coccidia will drain energy from a chinchilla, which can cause death.

Colds - Generally caused by variations in temperature, draughts, damp environments or stress.

Signs - Watery eyes with no inflammation, nasal discharge, sneezing, heavy breathing or wheezing,

Prevention - Keep a constant room temperature between 60-75 degrees Fahrenheit (15.5-24 °C) and ensure the cage is away from open windows, draughty places and out of damp, stressful environments.

Cures - Move the chinchilla to a warm, quiet room and ensure he/she eats and drinks plenty of water. Keep a close check on the chinchilla that the cold does not develop into pneumonia.

Fatality chance - MEDIUM-HIGH. Cured colds do not pose any threat to a chinchilla's health; it is only if it is neglected that a cold could develop into pneumonia, which can be fatal.

Constipation - Eating too many treats, improper or changes to the diet, not enough exercise and furballs (see Furballs) will cause a chinchilla to become constipated. Pregnant chinchillas in the latter stages of pregnancy are also prone to constipation.

Signs - Droppings will be small in size, dry, very hard, pointed and may smell. A chinchilla may become lethargic and pass droppings more slowly.

Prevention - Provide plenty of fresh water together with a healthy combination of pellets and hay. Regularly give your chinchilla alfalfa hay, which has more protein and is very fibrous. Only give the healthy treats in the correct quantities (see chapter on Diet and Feeding).

Cures - Increase exercise time and supply fresh water, hay and pellets, together with 1 raisin a day until the droppings have returned to normal. Go careful with constipation that you do not over feed and cause diarrhoea! Do not feed any treats apart from raisins and do so slowly.

Fatality Chance - HIGH. If left untreated constipation can develop into bowel paralysis or intestinal prolapse (see Intestinal Prolapse) eventually causing death.

Convulsions - Usually convulsions are triggered by calcium or vitamin B deficiency. Stress, head injuries, loud noises, pregnancy and genetic influences can all trigger convulsions. It can also be signs for latter stages of Listerious (*see Listerious*)

Signs - White teeth, muscle spasms, trembling, body contortion, jerky movements or temporary paralysis and dribbling.

Prevention - Ensure pregnant females are given a healthy diet and teeth are monitored regularly. Remove heights from the cage, which if falling from could hurt a chinchilla's head. When holding a chinchilla make sure you have a firm grasp so they do not wiggle out of your hands and fall to the floor. Feed good quality hay at all times.

Cures - Remove all objects that could possibly hurt the chinchilla and ensure the environment is safe. Call a vet immediately who may inject vitamin B to ease stress or some calcium. A chinchilla will need to be kept warm, in a quiet atmosphere and left alone (quiet observation is necessary).

Fatality Chance - HIGH. A vet will need to be called immediately as the chinchilla will be in a high state of shock and could potentially die. The chinchilla will need to be in a secure environment as to not further hurt itself and kept quiet and undisturbed. A constant vigil will be needed to ensure there are no further relapses.

Cryptosporidia - Highly infectious internal parasite as the eggs are contagious as soon as they are released (*see Parasites*). Cryptosporidia lives in the digestive system attacking the lining of the intestines, leaving harmful sores on the bodily organs. It can be caught from unclean cages and poor sanitation, unwashed hands after handling contaminated human food or a contaminated droppings entering the food bowl. Cryptosporidia can cause haemorrhages in older chinchillas and is highly contagious to humans.

Signs - Increased appetite, lethargy, diarrhoea (droppings extremely soft and easily mashed into shelves etc.), you may also notice blood in the droppings.

Prevention - Wash hands before handling chinchilla food, supply fresh pellets twice a day. Supply water that has been boiled and cooled for 20 minutes. Keep the cage in good sanitation and sterilise regularly. Probiotics added to water daily can also help.

Cures - A vet will need a fresh stool sample to examine and will prescribe medication in order to kill the parasites, usually a course over 5-7 days. Fresh boiled water will need to be supplied to help hydration after diahorrea. Complete sterilisation to the cage is paramount, using strong disinfectant and rinsing well with water. Anything that cannot be disinfected (i.e. wooden houses, carpets, wooden toys or hideaways) must be thrown away or replaced. Provide a fresh supply of pellets and hay (preferably alfalfa which has 18+ % protein to help build up the chinchilla)

Fatality Chance - HIGH. If untreated eventually cryptosporidium will drain energy from the chinchilla and cause death.

Cuts and Grazes- The ears and eyes of a chinchilla are susceptible to cuts and abrasions and act as a prime target when chinchillas start fighting. Dust or particulars entering a chinchilla's eye can be rubbed causing a scratch on the eyeball and inflammation.

Signs - Watery eyes, scratching of the area by the chinchilla, red and inflamed patches on chinchilla's skin.

Prevention - Do not give a chinchilla a dust bath if his eyes are wet, as dust will stick, making it easier to enter the eye socket and scratch the eyes. Any fighting chinchillas should be separated and re-introduced slowly. Check when cleaning the cage that there are no sharp objects in the cage that could scratch or injure a chinchilla.

Cures - Bathe the infected area with cold tea (black), twice a day until the infection has cleared up, you may put on some antiseptic cream/drops on the recommendation of your vet. A collar must be worn when using antiseptic cream so the chinchilla cannot get to the area and make it worse or consume the cream. Do not under any circumstances put antiseptic cream near the eye area. If a chinchilla needs vet analysis, a harmless fluorescent dye will be put into the chinchilla's eyes as this will show up any scratches under flourescent light, a vet will then prescribe the correct form of treatment.

Fatality Chance - LOW-MEDIUM. Providing the cuts or scratches are treated quickly infection should clear and no permanent ill effects should occur. Take the chinchilla to a vet if the cuts look deep or if you see no improvement after 3 days of bathing.

Depression - There can be many causes for depression and each source should be looked at and changed if the chinchilla is to change behaviour. Boredom, poor husbandry, loneliness, the onset of enteritis (see Enteritis), listeriosis (*see Listeriosis*) or other health issues can cause the onset of depression.

Signs - Lack of appetite, biting fur, unwillingness to play, unkept fur, lethargy, watery eyes, crouching in corners, teeth noises.

Prevention - Provide plenty of entertainment. If the chinchilla is a lone chinchilla perhaps think about obtaining another (see chapter on Introducing Chinchillas). Spend at least an hour a day playing and interacting with your chinchilla and ensure the cage is well kept at all times. If a chinchilla shows continual signs of depression it is best to sort a vets advice in case this is a symptom of a health concern.

Cures - If none of the prevention's shown above work, then it is best to take the chinchilla to a vet to check for bacterial infections to the GI tracts (see Internal Parasites).

Fatality Chance - MEDIUM-HIGH. If the symptoms are not recognised and are connected to something life threatening then a chinchilla can die.

Diabetes - Obese chinchillas can be prone to diabetes which is a disease disabling the body to produce or properly use insulin. Insulin is needed to aid the conversion of sugar, carbohydrates and other nutrients into energy for daily activity.

Signs - Loss of appetite, drooling, fruity smell to breath, over weight, lethargy, diarrhoea, excessive urination and coma. Collapsing after exercising.

Prevention - Provide plenty of exercise with a strict healthy diet and limited treats. A chinchilla should have a weight range between 400-600 grams (400-500 grams for a male and 500-600 grams for a female).

Cures - Try to get something sweet into the chinchilla if he/she collapses. The only cure will be provided by your vet in the form of insulin tablets/injections. You will need to carefully monitor food intakes and restrict treats.

Fatality Chance - HIGH. Diabetes will put a great strain on a chinchilla's system as you try to stabilise the blood sugar levels together with giving it daily injections/tablets for insulin. If you are not around when the chinchilla goes into hyperventilation the chinchilla will die.

Diarrhoea - A diet rich in treats, algae within the water bottle, mouldy or damp hay and quick changes in diet may all cause a bacterial infection known as diarrhoea.

Signs - Droppings will be soft (mushy), covered in a white mucus and will generally stick to where they land, they maybe smaller in size than healthy droppings. Weight loss will be apparent in the later stages.

Prevention - A healthy diet consisting of pellets, hay and water with limited amounts of treats will prevent diarrhoea. Ensure the treats you give him/her are of the correct type and amount (see chapter on Diet and Feeding) and never over feed a kit. Probiotics added to water will help keep the gut functioning normally and reguarly checking the teeth that they have not overgrown.

Cures - Stop all treats!. It is best to offer your chinchilla lots of fresh water and pellets until the symptoms clear. If this is an on-going problem you should take a fresh faeces sample to the vet to check for giardia, coccidian, or any other internal parasite or have the teeth filed.

Fatality Chance - HIGH - If the weight drops below 14oz (400grams) your chinchilla will become weak and may deteriorate. It is imperative that if the symptoms continue after 24 hours or you notice weight loss, you take the chinchilla to a vet immediately, as it will also be loosing vital fluids such as water and nutrients.

Drooling/Slobbering - (*see Malocclusion, Teeth, Excessive Wet Eye*)

Droppings - (*See Diarrhoea or Constipation*)

Ears - Should be clean and dry. Ear problems are quite rare in chinchillas but must be treated at first signs.

Signs - Watery discharge from the ear, pawing at ear, tipping head to one side, walking around in circles, loss of balance are all signs of an inner ear infection. A flaky ear is an indication of dry skin. Red veiny ears is a positive sign for elevated temperature or heat stroke (see Elevated Temperature and Heatsroke).

Prevention- Keep cages clean and ensure your chinchilla receives a regular dustbath. Any cuts or scratches to the ears should be treated immediately to prevent further infections. Once a week give your chinchilla two sunflower seeds to help replace oils and moisture to the ears.

Cures - For any infections take the chinchilla to a vet to administer antibiotics. You will need to ensure you continue the antibiotics at home to completely clear the infection. No dustbath should be given until the chinchilla is well again, usually 7-10 days. If the ears are scaly or flaky, cut back on the amount of dustbaths a week to help retain moisture.

Fatality chance - MEDIUM - A vet will need to administer antibiotics to treat the infection. If left untreated a chinchilla will become distressed, not eat and inevitably diminish. Scaly or flaky ears pose no threat to a chinchilla's life only aggravation.

Elevated Temperature - An elevated temperature is one of the first signs that something is wrong. It can be signs from a common cold to pneumonia or heat stoke (see Pneumonia and Heat-Stroke).

Signs - Ears will be bright pink and veiny. Fur will be damp and unkept. Signs of panting breath or lying on its side will be evident.

Prevention - Keep the chinchilla in good health, with a constant room temperature between 60-75 degrees Fahrenheit (15.5-24°C) and ensure the room is well ventilated. Never keep a chinchilla in sunlight or by a radiator.

Cures - Place a sealed tin containing iced water inside the cage for the chinchilla to lie against. You can also gently spray him/her with cold water to bring the temperature down but this may frighten him/her or as a final attempt, hold the chinchillas feet in some shallow cool water (not deep enough for him to drown) and allow the chinchilla to dry out on his own. Care should be taken when trying to cool a chinchilla in case he/she cools down too much and then becomes cold. If this happens you will need to reverse the process and place the chin in a warm room. Such fluctuations in temperature will not be good for your chinchilla's health so try not to leave him in cold water for more than 2 minutes.

Fatality Chance - HIGH. If untreated a chinchilla will die from heat stroke.

Enteritis - This is the medical name for infection of the digestive system. It prohibits a chemical reaction in the stomach and intestines that split complex compounds down to simple substances. This then leads to an overgrowth of bacteria. It is mainly caused by new diets, especially rich in protein and sugars, inactivity or stress. Medication or antibiotics can cause alterations in the fermentation process, which may continue to lead to enteritis. It can also be a generic inheritance of a dysfunctional digestive system.

Signs - Bloated and painful stomach/abdomen, loss of appetite, diarrhoea or constipation, lethargy leading to the unwillingness to move, partial paralysis, painful vocal sounds and teeth grinding, curling into a ball, depression or sudden death.

Prevention - A healthy diet with limited treats and a regularly cleaned cage. Medication or antibiotics should only be administered on the advice of a vet and monitored carefully for any side effects (see signs above). Probiotics added to water helps regulate the stomach.

Cures - Very hard to cure. First symptoms should be reported to your qualified vet immediately so safe antibiotics can begin to be administered if there is to be any chance of survival. Take a sample of their faeces with you when visiting the vet, as it will need to be determined which type of bacteria is present in order to administer the correct type of antibiotic. Extra water will need to be consumed to aid flushing the system and the present diet will need to be corrected. Only fresh hay and pellets should be given at this time and no treats! Constant attention will need to be given and you must ensure water is consumed even if you have to use a pipette.

Fatality Chance - VERY HIGH. Unfortunately enteritis is often fatal but noticing signs in the early stages may give the chinchilla a chance.

Epilepsy – A disorder of the brain and nervous system in which abnormal electrical activity in the brain causes seizures. Epilepsy can be caused by a number of things that make a difference in the way the brain works. Head injuries or lack of oxygen during birth may damage the delicate electrical system in the brain. Other causes include brain tumours, genetic conditions, animal testing and illnesses.

Signs - Abnormal movements or behaviour, stumbling, episodic loss of attention or sleepiness, sensory disturbance, confusion or severe convulsions with loss of consciousness.

Prevention - If seizures occur as the result of an underlying disease of the brain (e.g. a tumour) or body, treatment of these primary conditions can prevent seizures from occurring. Pre-Natal and Post-Natal care. If the chinchilla is having a fit, ensure he is in a safe environment where he cannot hurt himself until the fit is over or gently hold him in your hands.

Cure – A trip to the vet for diagnosis will be needed and medication administered although this can be harsh on the chinchilla's digestive tract.

Fatality Chance – MEDIUM-HIGH Generally an epileptic fit will not last long it's only if the chinchilla hurts himself in the process that the occurrence can prove dangerous.

Excessive Wet Eye (Tooth Root Elongation - See also Malocclusion & Teeth) - If a chinchilla's eye is constantly wet or watery it may be due to an overflow of tears medically known as lacrimal overflow. This is mainly caused by a blockage to the lacrimal canal usually adjacent to the root of the incisor tooth where the canal sharply changes direction. The blockage prohibits the entry of the tears into the nasal chamber of the nostril-causing overflow to be released in the eye socket. Tooth root elongation can also be a cause when the roots of the top row of teeth grow into the eye socket.

Signs - Excessive wet eyes and bumps under the eyes caused by root elongation.

Prevention - There are no preventative measures which can be taken against lacrimal overflow or tooth root elongation although a healthy fibrous diet and limited treats will ensure good nutrients are consumed by the chinchilla to aid development and growth.

Cures - Only a vet can rectify an obstruction via anaesthetic and surgery. A scan or x-ray of the facial area will be taken to identify any obstructions that will then need to be surgically removed or corrected.

Fatality Chance - HIGH. Incisor roots can be long in a chinchilla and when in contact with the lacrimal canal it can puncture the walls and enter the system causing fatal consequences to the chinchilla's health.

Eye Infection - (*see Watery Eyes*)

Feet (Flaky or Scabby) - (*see Fungus Infection*)

Fever - (*see Heat-Stroke and Elevated Temperature*)

Fleas - It is very rare for a flea to reach the skin of a chinchilla due to their dense fur. In extremely rare cases fleas can be caught from living in the outdoor environment or home that is infested with fleas from other animals.

Signs - Constant itching and nibbling at the area, jumping around cage, anxious and un-relaxed.

Prevention - Keep the chinchilla away from the outside environment and at bay from other pets.

Cures - A trip to the vet for some flea powder. The cage will need to be completely disinfected and treated as will all areas the chinchilla has come into contact with.

Fatality Chance - LOW. It will be extremely hard for a flea to get within an ears reach of the chinchillas skin but if it does it will not be harmful as long as they are treated effectively and quickly.

Frozen Tail - This condition is generally caused by outside housing or housing in unheated conditions.

Signs - The tail becomes paralysed and rigid.

Prevention - Keep the living quarters at a warm, constant temperature between 60-75 degrees Fahrenheit (15.5-24°C) and never house a chinchilla outside unless the living quarters are heated.

Cures - Unfortunately, unless caught straight away the tail usually drops off. Bring the chinchilla into a warm room immediately, if you wish you could dip the tail in warm (not hot!) water but not the whole body, as this will shock the system too quickly. Apply a collar so the chinchilla will not chew the tail and if the worst happens and the tail detaches call a vet to administer anti inflammatory tablets, do not rub, dry or warm the tail in your hands as it can easily break off when frozen.

Fatality Chance - LOW-MEDIUM. A chinchilla will not die from frozen tail, it just generally drops off and there is not a significant blood loss to be concerned about. The main concern where this could turn fatal is if infection sets in to the large open area or the chinchilla starts chewing the wound. Even so, it is wise to seek a vets advice at the first signs of frozen tail to ensure you are doing all you can to save it.

Fungus - Fungus infections irritate the top layer of the skin before infecting lower layers. Dark, damp, stagnant and unclean cages are prone to fungus that will attack a chinchilla's health. It can appear at any time but mainly during the hot and humid summer months.

Signs - The moist areas of a chinchilla will be affected first. The eyes will become watery, inflamed and scabby with loss of hair, the nose area will loose fur and show red, inflamed skin underneath and whiskers may be broken, split or bent. The overall body will display clumps of missing fur with red, inflamed patches of skin underneath. Feet can also become scabby and flaky. Fungus is contagious therefore regular washing of hands should always follow handling an infected chinchilla.

Prevention - Fungus infections are air-bone therefore always ensure the cage is dry, well lit, has good ventilation and is disinfected regularly. The cage should be cleaned at least once a week to prevent fungus growing. Two teaspoons of anti fungal powder can be added to the dust bath once a month to keep skin fungus at bay.

Cures - The cage must be completely disinfected to disperse off any fungus/mites or other parasites already present and 2 teaspoons of anti-fungal powder (athletes foot powder) should be added to the dust bath. If signs are chronic, apply anti-fungal powder direct to the affected areas, apart from the eyes until all symptoms have gone. You can use a collar on the chinchilla to prevent scabby feet touching eyes to restrain eye infection.

Fatality Chance - MEDIUM. Fungus and mites are parasites that attack a chinchilla over time and the severity will be shown in the appearance. It is unlikely that you would leave the chinchilla in this condition so symptoms should clear with no further effects.

Furballs - Chinchillas love to groom themselves and just like cats can accumulate furballs in their stomachs and intestines. Unlike cats, chinchillas cannot vomit; therefore furballs become stuck in the intestines and cause constipation (*see Constipation*) or worse bowel paralysis and intestinal prolapse (*see Intestinal Prolapse*).

Signs - Droppings will be small in size, dry, very hard, pointed and may smell. A chinchilla may become lethargic and pass droppings more slowly.

Prevention - Luckily fur balls are not common, as there are no real preventative actions apart from grooming your chinchilla's fur. Not all chinchillas will be happy about this so compensate with a high fibrous diet - hay will aid bowel movements therefore it should be readily available at all times.

Cures - Fresh papaya juice (diluted), papaya enzyme and pineapple juice have been stated as helping a chinchilla pass furballs, never administer any of this without prior consent from the vet for recommended dosages.

Fatality Chance - HIGH. If untreated furballs will cause severe constipation and can develop into paralysis of the bowel or intestinal prolapse.

Fur Biting - This is a genetic or stress related behaviour. It can have many different causes such as: crowded living quarters, dietary imbalances, noisy environment in daytime, boredom, loneliness, skin irritation (*see Fungus Infection*) or inheritance from parents.

Signs - Bald patches or short/cut fur (short hair should not be mistaken for shedding (*see Shedding*)), usually seen on the hind leg area, stomach or lower back.

Prevention - Provide toys and activities for the chinchilla, also allow the chinchilla more time out of the cage to run around. Keep the cage in a room that is unused within the daytime and provide a nutritional balanced diet (*see chapter on Diet and Feeding*). Do not overload the cage with accessories so there is plenty of room for the chinchilla to run about freely.

Cures - There are no real cures for fur biting, it has been the mystery of many chinchilla owners for years. Try all the prevention methods first, if they do not work the chinchilla may be lonely if living on its own. Either spend more quality time or consider purchasing a second mate, do this as a last resort and only if you are familiar with the responsibilities (*see Introducing Chinchillas and Breeding Chinchillas*) but remember it may not be successful and you could end up with two fur chewers!

Fatality Chance - LOW. Fur biting is generally a behaviour related illness and should not affect the actual health of the chinchilla only its fur.

Fur Loss - Fur loss can be caused by stress, fighting, shedding (*see chapter on Shedding*) or by holding a chinchilla in an incorrect manner. Chinchillas have a built in defence mechanism to release fur if caught by a predator; this in the wild would have given the chinchilla an opportunity to escape to freedom. (*Also see Fur Biting & Fungus Infection*).

Signs - Bald patches all around the body with no red skin infection.

Prevention - Separate aggressive animals if fighting causes fur loss. Find and eliminate the cause for stress and keep the chinchilla in a quiet calm room. Should fur loss be down to handling or catching the chinchilla in an incorrect manner, relearn the steps of handling and catching shown by consulting the relevant sections of this book.

Cures - There is no cure for fur loss apart from prevention. Fur will return to full-length within 4-6 months.

Fatality Chance - LOW. No harm will come to a chinchilla with fur loss.

Giardia - Giardia is an internal parasite (*see Internal Parasite*) within the small intestine, which attaches its sucker-like mouth to internal mucus. Contamination is oral or faeces based and can be passed to a chinchilla via unwashed hands after handing contaminated human food or a contaminated dropping entering the food bowl.

Signs - Increased appetite, lethargy, diarrhoea (droppings will be extremely soft and easily mashed into shelves etc.), bloating.

Prevention - Wash hands before handling chinchilla food and provide a fresh supply of pellets twice a day. Supply water that has been boiled and cooled for 20 minutes.

Cures - A vet will need to prescribe medication in order to kill the parasites and will usually be a course over 5-7 days. Take the chinchilla and fresh faeces with you to be examined. Cooled boiled water will need to be supplied to help hydration after diahorrhea. Complete sterilisation to the cage using strong disinfectant and washed well with water. Anything that cannot be sterilised (i.e. wooden houses or hideaways) must be thrown away or replaced. Provide a fresh supply of pellets and hay (preferably alfalfa which has 18+ % protein to

help build up the chinchilla).
Fatality Chance - HIGH. If untreated eventually giardia will drain energy from the chinchilla and cause death.

Hair-ring (paraphimosis) - This condition mainly occurs during mating but can occur at anytime and only affects the male. Loose hair is wrapped around the penis causing paraphimosis - swelling of the penis causing the inability to retract back into the foreskin.
Signs - The penis will be seen outside the foreskin. The male will constantly be attending to this region trying to get the hair off, other signs are loss of appetite, sitting in a different position and finding it hard to walk (advanced stages).
Prevention - Check the male periodically and after mating by gently pulling out the penis (approx. 1") from the foreskin inspecting for hair wrapped around the shaft. You can also give the chinchilla a treat, holding it high up so he needs to be on his hindlegs to receive it, this way you will be able to see his penis without handling him for a basic inspection.
Cures - If hair is present it will need to be removed immediately. Very very gently massage an unscented lubricant around the shaft and slowly try and ease off the hair. When all hair is removed very gently push the penis back into the foreskin. If the swelling has become chronic, you can put ice in a towel or use a towel that has been soaked in cold water and gently hold it to the penis for 10-15 minutes every 2-3 hours until the swelling has reduced. Ensure you keep the area lubricated using petroleum jelly to help reverse the cracking and drying out effect the hair ring may cause. Keep an eye on the chinchilla afterwards to ensure no further inflammation occurs, if the male is constantly licking the infected the area, you can apply a collar to stop him reaching it. Removal of the hair ring must be done very carefully if no harm is to come to the chinchilla's penis, it is very delicate and can cause further complications if damaged, therefore if you do not feel comfortable doing this yourself call a vet immediately!

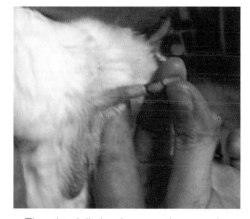

This chinchilla has hair ring that must be removed immediately.

Fatality chance - VERY HIGH - Serious medical condition which needs prompt attention. If not treated straight away urine will accumulate in the shaft and inflammation will occur causing swelling. The penis will begin to dry up and crack and cause agonising pain. Eventually, pressure build-up of urine will cause fluid to ooze out of the penis and foreskin. Severe cases will mean amputation to the penis.

Heart Murmurs - These are the irregular sounds of the heartbeat and is the result of blood flowing in both directions. It can be caused by weakened heart muscles and valves. It can be genetic or developed through lack of essential minerals. It is essential that you do not breed a chinchilla with heart murmurs
Signs - When listening to the heartbeat via a stethoscope, irregular beats will be heard. Unfortunately there are no visual signs to a heart murmur.
Prevention - Good exercise to strengthen the heart muscles and vowels. A diet containing nutrients such as Vitamin C or calcium.
Cures - Strengthening the heart and the values will help the murmur and protect against heart attack. Ensure the chinchilla has ample time to exercise alternatively purchase a safe chinchilla wheel that has a flat running surface so not to catch those toes!
Fatality Chance - MEDIUM. Providing a chinchilla is put on a healthy diet mainly of pellets and hay and is given free time out of the cage to develop the respiratory system and muscles of the heart, there is no reason why a chinchilla can not live a normal healthy long life. Leaving a chinchilla without exercise and attention will cause the muscles of the heart to get weaker raising the chances of a heart attack.

Heat Stroke - Temperatures of 75+ degrees Fahrenheit (24+°C) accompanied by high humidity can lead to fatal heat stroke in the chinchilla. As chinchillas cannot sweat, like humans, high volumes of exercise in warm temperatures can also give a chinchilla heat stroke. The lungs become congested causing the chinchilla to have difficulties in breathing and fluid may appear in the nose and mouth.
Signs - Panting with open mouth, sweating, lethargy, lying on its side, ears will be red and veins protruding, unkept damp fur.
Prevention - Keep room temperature between 60-75 degrees Fahrenheit and well ventilated. Never keep the cage in sunlight or near a radiator. In warm climates ensure there is a metal tin with frozen water placed inside the cage. With the lid on the tin, you will find any over heating chinchillas will lie on top or around the side of the tin to cool off. Never over exercise your pet when the climate is warm; always keep vigorous exercises to 15-20 minute intervals. If you need to travel with your chinchilla, ensure he has a well-ventilated cage and the transport has windows open. Never place the cage on the floor of transport as it can get a lot hotter down there!
Cures - Chinchillas should be cooled down slowly to prevent seizure. First place the chinchilla in a cooler room, with plenty of ventilation. Alternatively, gently spray your chinchilla with cold water or carefully pick the chinchilla up and dip its body into cool water (not freezing!) for 2 minutes or as long as the chinchilla can bear it, do not submerge its head! As they cannot regulate their own body temperature, ensure the temperature does not drop below its natural body level (between 96-100 degrees Fahrenheit) especially after cooling.

Leave the wet chinchilla to dry out on his own. Directing a fan into the cage will not bring the chinchillas temperature down only circulate the air and it may cause conjunctivas or a cold.

Fatality Chance - VERY HIGH - If unattended your chinchilla will die! If you treat the chinchilla immediately and his temperature returns to normal, there will be no permanent side effects; Never place a chinchilla in cold water, this will cause shock or seizure, only use cool water!

Intestinal Prolapse - Is a severe case of constipation. A chinchilla can force the droppings out together with its intestines which is known as intestinal prolapse.

Signs - Serious constipation in a chinchilla with no droppings passed for 12 hours are first signs.

Prevention - Keep a close eye on a chinchilla that has constipation, ensure it has plenty of water and feed it 2 raisins immediately.

Cures - There are no cures for intestinal prolapse apart from a vet's immediate help. Never ever try and push the intestines back yourself!

Fatality Chance - VERY HIGH. This is a life-threatening situation so call a vet immediately. Do not pick up a chinchilla in this state, as it will cause it to panic. Ask the vets advise on how to transport the animal to the surgery and follow all instructions carefully!

Internal Worms - Hookworms, roundworm, tapeworms, pinworms are all parasites which can live within the GI tract of a chinchilla and decrease the absorption of nutrients from digested food. It is generally caught from contaminated food or water and unhygienic living quarters.

Signs - Increased appetite, lethargy, diarrhoea-sometimes worms can be visible in faeces and may look like grains of rice or seeds. In severe cases a chinchilla may bloat up.

Prevention - Wash hands before handling chinchilla food and supply fresh pellets twice a day. Provide water that has been boiled and cooled for 20 minutes. Keep cages in good sanitation and sterilise regularly.

Cures - A cure is only possible via a qualified vet. You will need to take your chinchilla with you so it can provide fresh faeces to be tested.

Fatality Chance - HIGH. Lack of vital nutrients will cause a chinchilla to lose weight and eventually starve to death.

Isolation - Chinchillas do not generally live well on their own unless there is constant attention from the owner. In the wild they live in colonies of up to 100 and preferably should always be paired with a mate.

Signs - Depression, listlessness, loss of fur, fur biting and loss of appetite.

Prevention - Provide good entertainment for your chinchilla, spend quality time each night interacting and keep them in pairs, Give good quality feed and never ignore your chinchilla.

Cures - Try to keep chinchillas in pairs and if you have a lone chinchilla ensure you put quality time aside every night to interact with your pet to prevent deterioration.

Fatality Chance - MEDIUM - A chinchilla will not die from being on its own but it will start to show signs of social and behavioural problems if there is no interaction.

Listeriosis - Can cause death at any time and can be common amongst chinchillas. It is bacteria based affecting the liver and is highly infectious to humans therefore care should be taken by washing your hands before and after contact. It is usually acquired orally via another infected chinchilla or through hay that has been in contact with an infected mouse etc. before processing.

Signs - Develops slowly and spreads to other chinchillas. Diarrhoea or constipation will be visible and a chinchilla may show signs of nervousness by shaking its head. Just prior to death, blindness can lead to a chinchilla bumping into objects and an unwillingness to move unless urged. Finally they will show signs of pain by making vocal sounds, stop feeding (although they may continue their water consumption) and grind their teeth.

Prevention - Listeriosis can develop through poor sanitation therefore it is imperative that cages, equipment, dustbaths and waterholders are disinfected regularly. Check the hay sources that you buy and introduce new chinchillas cautiously if you do not know their background. Never touch droppings as the bacteria are passed through the faeces and are highly infectious.

Cures - Administration of antibiotics should be given immediately by a vet if there is any chance of recovery. If left to become seriously infected a chinchilla may have to be put to sleep (euthanasia). A cured chinchilla may still be a carrier of the bacteria therefore further care should be taken when handling the chinchilla and never introduce him/her to others. Wash and disinfect the cage, equipment and anywhere the chinchilla has made contact with.

Fatality Chance - VERY HIGH. Not all chinchillas will respond to antibiotics therefore if there is any chance for a chinchilla to survive, listeriosis will need to be diagnosed in its early stages. Ensure any antibiotics are fully consumed as some placed in water may not be fully digested or may even be disregarded by you pet.

Liver Failure - (*see Severe Hunchback*)

Malocclusions (*see also Teeth*) - Is a faulty connection between the upper and lower jaws when meeting and is usually caused by genetics, overgrown molars or lack of certain minerals. When teeth become loose in their sockets or the mouth is hit from falling, teeth can become misaligned - instead of pointing straight up or down they lean at a slight angle - this can cause uneven wear. Eventually spurs may form - these can be sharp, grow fast and inflict cuts to the mouth & tonque causing pain when eating. A spur can also continue to grow through the mouth wall causing immense pain. Tooth Root Elongation can also develop where the roots of the upper teeth grow into the eye sockets and the roots of the lower teeth grow into the jaw. It is essential that you do not breed a chinchilla with malocclusion.

Signs - A chinchilla will not be able to close its jaws properly, causing difficulty in eating, wetness around the mouth area and loss in weight due to the inability to feed. You will also see ungroomed clumps of fur around the thigh area, bumps under the eyes or along the jawbone.

Prevention - Provide hard toys to chew and file teeth. A good nutritional diet containing a Calcium supplement as described by your vet. (i.e. Tums tablet) may help. Good quality hay to help file the teeth and promote proper side-to-side chewing motion.

Cures - If the condition is a case of overgrown molars, these can be filed under anaesthetic by your vet, also whilst under anaesthetic your vet may wish to take an x-ray to check the alignment of the jaw bone and check the top and bottom layers of teeth connect properly. A course of calcium supplements may be recommended.

Fatality Chance - HIGH. If left a chinchilla will starve to death. It is a common complaint that can occasionally be prevented by providing correct diet and hard chewing toys.

Medications - Should be administered with caution and only with the guidance of a qualified vet. As chinchillas have a sensitive GI tract it is wise to look out for any side effects from medication and report them straight to the administering vet. Should medication be necessary it is best to avoid any that need to be sprinkled on food as this is not fully consumed and harder to monitor. Medication in the form of a tablet can be hidden in treats, such as the middle of a raisin or sandwiched in an apple ring (although it will not take long for a chinchilla to 'suss' you out and refuse the treat). Oral medication can be diluted and

Ellis – Pure Standard, Male being hand feed.

either given in a pipette or added to unsweetened Cranberry juice. Go careful administering medications via a pipette to avoid choking or over feeding causing bloating.

Mites - (*see Fungus Infections*)

Nasal Duct Blockage - (*see Wet Eye*)

Parasites (External) - (*see Fungus Infections*)

Parasites (Internal) - Common to the GI tract and includes coccidian, cryptosporidium, and giardia (*see respective descriptions*). Internal parasites feed from passing food, taking vital nutrients, which to a growing kit will be detrimental to its development and to an older chinchilla deterioration of health.
Signs - Increased appetite, lethargy, diarrhoea (droppings will be extremely soft and easily mashed into the shelves of the cage etc.), faeces may show signs of blood. At later stages, signs of bloating will become apparent.
Prevention - Wash hands before handling chinchilla food and provide a fresh supply of pellets twice a day. Give water that has been boiled and cooled and add probiotics to regulate the gut. Keep cages in good sanitation and sterilise regularly.
Cures - If water supply is the problem you can use an extra fine filter system or boil the water and allow to cool.
Fatality Chance - HIGH. If left untreated a chinchilla will be robbed of vital nutrients that can affect development and cause starvation leading to death.

Pneumonia - This condition is caused by an infection of the respiratory system. Untreated colds, draughty and dusty places or bacterial agents such as Pasteurella, Pseudomonas, Bordetella or E-Coli within the air and hay can cause it. It has a devastating effect on the breathing system and places unusual stress on the heart and respiratory system.
Signs - Wet watery eyes with no infection, wet nose and loss of appetite. An elevated temperature will also be shown in the ears that will be bright pink and veiny, feeling unusually warm to the touch. Wheezing and panting for breath are both indications of pneumonia.
Prevention - Ensure symptoms of a cold clear within a few days, and keep the cage in a clean, dry, dust/draught free area.
Cures - Antibiotics administered via a vet is the only cure. Ensure the cage is well ventilated.
Fatality Chance - HIGH. If pneumonia is untreated respiratory failure will occur causing death to the chinchilla. If the symptoms are treated early no prolonged effect should take place and the respiratory system will return to normal functions.

Ringworm - Ringworm is a fungal infection (*see Fungus Infections*) and affects the dead cells on the top layer of skin causing fur loss and scabby red sores around the eyes, nose and feet.

Signs - Fur loss will be apparent with exposing pink-red rashes sometimes forming round patches with a clear centre that can be weepy or runny. Mainly effects the moist areas of the body but can generally spread to all areas.
Prevention - (*see Fungus Infections*)
Cures - A chinchilla will need to visit a vet for medication, Griseofulvin has been used in the past to help cure this problem. (*see Fungus Infections*).
Fatality Chance - (*see Fungus Infections*).

Seizures - (*see Convulsions*)

Severe Hunchback - Hunchback is a specific indication of a liver problem or inflammation of the bowel (bowel disease) and is caused by improper diet of high sugar, proteins and fats etc. or can be genetic.
Signs - Easily noticeable when a chinchilla is sitting sidewards as the back and shoulders will be hunched up giving the illusion that the back of the neck is sunken.
Prevention - Proper proportions of nutrients (*see chapter on Diet and Feeding*) should be provided with limited treats and constant supply of fresh water.
Cures - Only a vet can help. If the symptoms are due to bowel disease a vet may give you a course of antibiotics, either way diagnosis will need to be done via x-ray.
Fatality Chance - VERY HIGH. A serious illness that needs immediate attention, it is possible to cure at early stages but if left will lead to liver failure and death.

Shock - Can be brought on by a multitude of things but is usually due to a loud sudden noise or a large pet being introduced into the family. Other causes can arise from being dropped, being put into a cage of another without proper introductions or being taken from its home environment or owner.
Signs - A chinchilla will remain extremely still, almost paralysed. Ongoing shock will lead to loss of fur, appetite, weakness and in serious cases death.
Prevention - Keep the chinchilla's home in a quiet location away from sudden noises or busy activities. Introduce new pets gradually and if going on holiday find a baby sitter and do not uproot your pet to a new environment. I know of someone who has come back from holiday to find her chinchilla completely bald due to its owners absence and the chinchillas elevated stress levels.
Cures - Remove the source of the shock and give your pet a treat to check he/she is reacting OK, if so, place a dust bath in the cage and leave well alone. Check on the chinchilla a few minutes later to see if it has returned to normal activity. If you cannot get a positive result from your pet, call a vet immediately.
Fatality Chance - MEDIUM-HIGH. Generally shock is short lived and you

should be able to bring the effected chinchilla around with calm influences. If the shock is ongoing the pet will most certainly deteriorate and die.

Skin Irritations - (*see Fungus Infection*)

Teeth (*also see Malocclusion & Excessive Wet Eye*) – Problems can occur at anytime and is the most common problem in chinchillas. Teeth grow continually and should be yellow-orange in colour. Each tooth needs an opposing tooth to ensure even wear. White coloured teeth indicate lack of calcium and other potential health issues. Top teeth should be slightly shorter than bottom teeth. Problems can be fatal if untreated, as the teeth will be left to grow and can puncture any part of the inside of the mouth. Tooth root elongation can also be another problem when the roots of the lower teeth grow into the jaw or the roots from the upper teeth may grow upwards into the eye sockets (*see Excessive Wet Eye*). Malocclusion is another tooth problem where the top and bottom rows of teeth are not aligned properly (*see Malocclusion*).

Signs - Watering eyes, dribbling and wet fur around mouth, pawing at the mouth when eating, ungroomed fur around back of the chinchillas legs, loss of appetite and weight loss will also be apparent. Bumps under eye sockets or bumps along jawbone. Vocal sounds can also be heard

Prevention - The main cause of overgrown teeth is a lack of fibre in the diet, minimum chewing material and trauma to the mouth (maybe from being hit when falling – *see Malocclusion*). It is essential that a chinchilla has plenty of hard toys such as pumice stone, pebbles, tree branches etc. to aid filing of the front teeth. The most essential prevention is good quality tough fibrous hay. The side-to-side chewing motion promotes even filing of the teeth. Diet is essential for the formation of healthy teeth. 6 monthly vet check ups with a qualified vet who can check a chinchillas teeth/mouth without administering anaesthetic.

Cures – Take the chinchilla to a vet to get the teeth filed or x-rayed, this will need to be done under anaesthetic to stop the chinchilla from stressing out and will need to be done on a regular 6-8 week basis. Readjust diet and add toys to help file teeth.

Fatality chance – HIGH. If a chinchilla is not eating either because the teeth are too long or due to another illness he/she will starve and ultimately die. Should a vet file the teeth then no further problems should occur.

Tooth Spur - (*See Malocclusion + Excessive Wet Eye*)

Vaccinations - There are no common vaccinations on the market for chinchillas. Although there are some offered to breeders against bacterial infections that could potentially wipe out their whole breed.

Watery Eyes - The eyes should be bright, clear and dry. Eyes are extremely good at indicating a chinchilla's present health. If you feel your chinchilla is unwell, one place to look at is its eyes.

A dry and shiny eye is one indicator of a chinchillas good health.

Signs - Dull watery eyes accompanied with infection (inflamed swollen lids with white discharge) either indicates conjunctivitis that can be contagious or dust, woodshavings, hay particles stuck in the eyes. Watery eyes with loss of fur will diagnose fungus (*see Fungus*). Watery eyes with no inflammation indicate improper diet (*see chapter on Diet and Feeding*), stress (*see Stress*), a cold (*see Cold*), pneumonia (*see Pneumonia*), blockage to the nasal duct (*see Excessive Wet Eye*) or teeth problems (*see Teeth/Malocclusion*).

Prevention - To prevent any infections caused by dust, woodshavings etc, it is advisable to clean the cage on a more regular basis therefore keeping flying particles to a minimum. Prevention for other causes are indicated under the respective topics within the Health Guide.

Cures - Give the chinchilla an eyewash of either cold tea (no milk and sugar please!) or luke-warm water twice a day until the symptoms clear. If the symptoms have not cleared within 3 days take the chinchilla to a vet who will check his/her teeth or prescribe antibiotic drops (drops should always be asked for as they will enter straight into the eye socket and will be easier to administer than cream).

Fatality Chance - HIGH. If the cause is left untreated and it is an indication of stress, cold, pneumonia or teeth issues then a chinchilla will die. Conjunctivitis and infections can be treated and no further problems should occur with the eyes.

Weight Loss (*See also Teeth*) - A healthy chinchilla should weigh between 400-600 grams (14-21ounces). A chinchilla under 300 grams (10½ ounces) is unlikely to survive due to progressive weakness. There are many causes that will need to be immediately addressed if a chinchilla is to gain weight and survive. Serious illnesses that will cause weight loss are: malocclusion, diarrhoea, hair ring, depression, isolation and teeth issues.

Signs - Gradual loss of weight, protruding bones, watery eyes, lethargy, unwillingness to eat and depression will all be apparent.

Prevention - Ensure all preventions for individual causes are intact and your chinchilla is weighed regularly. (If your chinchilla is hard to handle it will help if you place some weighing scales on the floor of the cage, the chinchilla will soon jump on them and weigh themselves). Also have the teeth checked regularly by a vet who can look into the chinchillas mouth without the need to anaesthatise.

Cures - Some owners have been known to feed their chinchillas sugared water through a pipette to induce eating and occasionally it has been successful, (1part sugar: 4parts water), although care must be taken as to not induce diarrhoea. I would always recommend you seek immediate vet attention for a chinchilla with weight loss, it is not worth making your own diagnosis and getting it wrong. Follow the advice given and ensure you monitor regularly for any weight gain.

Fatality Chance - HIGH. Usually a sign of the latter stages of ill health therefore a chinchilla should be taken to the vet straight away if any signs of weight loss appear.

White teeth - Chinchilla's teeth should be yellow-orange, if your chinchilla has white teeth it means he is lacking in calcium which can lead to seizures and brain damage.

Signs - White or creamy teeth!

Prevention - A good healthy diet, with extra calcium in the form of 1 Tums tablet daily is a good prevention.

Cures - See prevention shown above.

Fatality Chance - MEDIUM. Although white teeth cannot kill a chinchilla its effects can. If a chinchilla continues to lack calcium in severe cases its teeth will become weak and break and the chinchilla will eventually starve to death.

X-rays - Should not be performed regularly on a chinchilla, as it has to be anaesthetised causing immense stress and potential death if not administered in a small amount.

INTERESTING WEBSITES

http://www.etc-etc.com/1926art.htm article appearing in an issue of Nature Magazine from December 1926!

http://www.etc-etc.com/1933art.htm article appearing in an issue of Popular Science Monthly from December 1933!

Origination
http://www.etc-etc.com/chapman.htm (Chapman story)

The Chinchilla
http://www.lsu.edu/deafness/HearingRange.html hearing range

Chinchilla Colouring
http://www.geocities.com/chinchillacrazyuk/pictures.htm#mutations colours

Chinchilla Genetics & Creating Colours
http://members.aol.com/UHChins/UnderhillChinchillas/breedfound.htm
http://www.chin.buffnet.net/

Raising Kits
http://members.aol.com/sirchin/breed.htm#babiescare kit birth weight

Health Guide
http://members.aol.com/sirchin/health1.htm health guide
http://www.geocities.com/Petsburgh/Park/6920/problem.html health guide

USEFUL CONTACT NUMBERS IN THE UK

Chinchilla Chat Line (C.C.L.)
www.chinchat.net

Tel: 01752 256053 Roger Wear (Author/Director of C.C.L)
       01902 829802 Liz Smith

INDEX